REPORT

T0119390

Reserve Recruiting and the College Market

Is a New Educational Benefit Needed?

Beth Asch, David Loughran

Prepared for the Office of the Secretary of Defense

RAND NATIONAL DEFENSE RESEARCH INSTITUTE

The research described in this report was sponsored by the Office of the Secretary of Defense (OSD). The research was conducted in the RAND National Defense Research Institute, a federally funded research and development center supported by the OSD, the Joint Staff, the unified commands, and the defense agencies under Contract DASW01-01-C-0004.

Library of Congress Cataloging-in-Publication Data

Asch, Beth J.
    Reserve recruiting and the college market : is a new educational benefit needed? / Beth Asch, David Loughran.
       p. cm.
    Includes bibliographical references.
    "TR-127."
    ISBN 0-8330-3686-6 (pbk. : alk. paper)
    1. United States—Armed Forces—Reserves. 2. United States—Armed Forces—Recruiting, enlistment, etc.
3. United States—Armed Forces—Pay, allowances, etc. 4. College students—Employment—United States.
I. Loughran, David S., 1969– II. Title.

UA42.A73 2005
378.3'2—dc22

                                                                                    2004023938

The RAND Corporation is a nonprofit research organization providing objective analysis and effective solutions that address the challenges facing the public and private sectors around the world. RAND's publications do not necessarily reflect the opinions of its research clients and sponsors.

RAND® is a registered trademark.

Published 2005 by the RAND Corporation
1776 Main Street, P.O. Box 2138, Santa Monica, CA 90407-2138
1200 South Hayes Street, Arlington, VA 22202-5050
201 North Craig Street, Suite 202, Pittsburgh, PA 15213-1516
RAND URL: http://www.rand.org/
To order RAND documents or to obtain additional information, contact
Distribution Services: Telephone: (310) 451-7002;
Fax: (310) 451-6915; Email: order@rand.org

PREFACE

The success of the active and reserve components in meeting their national defense missions is contingent on their ability to attract and retain high-quality personnel. Recruiting for the active components has become more challenging as the proportion of high school graduates seeking to attend college directly after high school has increased. Studies of active duty recruiting find that potential high-quality recruits view military service as a substitute for college attendance, not a complement. In an effort to make military service more complementary with college attendance, the active components have enhanced existing educational benefit programs and experimented with new enlistment programs in which enlistees attend college first and serve on active duty second. How the heightened interest in college attendance among American youth has impacted reserve recruiting is less clear. In general, reservists can and do attend college while serving in the Reserves. Some potential recruits, however, may wish to pursue college more intensively than is permitted by a reserve career, especially when one considers the increasing likelihood that a reservist's academic studies will be interrupted by activation.

The RAND Corporation was asked to assess whether new programs, such as those offered by some active components, would help the reserve components meet their current and future recruiting goals with respect to high-quality non-prior and prior service recruits. The findings of this project, entitled "Reserve Recruiting and the College Market" are reported in this document. The report is intended to inform policymakers and should be of interest to researchers and policy analysts concerned with military recruiting.

This research was sponsored by the Office of the Undersecretary of Defense for Personnel and Readiness and conducted within the Forces and Resources Policy Center of the RAND National Defense Research Institute, a federally funded research and development center sponsored by the Office of the Secretary of Defense, the Joint Staff, the Unified

Combatant Commands, the Department of the Navy, the Marine Corps, the defense agencies, and the defense Intelligence Community.

For more information on RAND's Forces and Resources Policy Center, contact the Director, James Hosek. He can be reached by e-mail at james_hosek@rand.org; by phone at 310-393-0411, extension 7183; or by mail at the RAND Corporation, 1776 Main Street, Santa Monica, California 90407-2138. More information about RAND is available at www.rand.org.

CONTENTS

FIGURES AND TABLES

FIGURES

TABLES

SUMMARY

Like the active components, the reserve components seek to attract and retain high-quality individuals to meet their enlistment requirements. These high-quality youth are increasingly interested in obtaining a college degree, making it more difficult for the active and reserve components to meet their enlistment goals. Today, about two-thirds of high school graduates enroll in college within a year of graduation. Rising college enrollment has put colleges in direct competition with the active components for high-quality high school graduates. In response, the active components of the Navy and Army have developed new recruiting programs that allow enlistees to attend college before assuming the duties of active military personnel. These recruiting programs represent a significant departure from the traditional educational incentives offered to potential enlistees, such as Montgomery GI Bill (MGIB) benefits that fund college after, not before, an enlistee fulfills his or her enlistment obligation.

Whether rising college enrollment puts college attendance in direct competition with the reserve components is less clear. On one hand, individuals can easily join a reserve unit while attending college because reservists are generally only obligated to drill one weekend per month and two weeks during the summer. On the other hand, reserve participation entails an increasingly high risk of activation of uncertain length. Individuals who want to attend college full time and finish quickly may believe that such a risk is unacceptable.

RAND was asked to provide a preliminary assessment of whether new programs, such as those offered by some active components, could help the reserve components attract high-quality recruits, with prior or non-prior service, and whether the potential of these programs warrants a more extensive evaluation, including randomized field trials. The findings of our study are summarized in this report.

The approach we take to this assessment is largely qualitative and descriptive; we do not explicitly test how a new educational benefit program would affect reserve recruiting. In this report, we first review

the evidence on the rising demand for a college education among
America's youth in general and among reservists themselves, and we ask
whether the composition of college students in terms of aptitude has
changed over time. The composition of the college-bound population and
how it is changing is relevant to the issue of designing educational
benefits that appeal to this population. Second, we examine how
reservists currently combine reserve service with college attendance and
civilian employment and describe how the nature of college attendance
has changed over time and varies according to cognitive ability. This
evidence provides an indication of the extent to which potential
recruits might view reserve duty as interfering with their civilian work
and college plans.

Third, we review the principal types of educational benefits
available to reservists and provide information on their usage and on
how satisfied reservists are with those benefits. We also compare the
educational benefits available to reservists with those available to
civilians and other military personnel. While the adequacy of existing
educational benefits must ultimately be judged on the basis of whether
they cost-effectively improve high-quality accessions in the reserve
components, the review of these programs and comparisons with benefits
available to other individuals provides a useful starting point in that
assessment. Finally, we synthesize the descriptive analyses of the
college market, the way in which reservists combine work and college,
and the educational benefits currently available to reservists in order
to provide a preliminary assessment of whether a restructured reserve
educational benefit is likely to affect reserve enlistments.

MAIN FINDINGS

Our description of the college market focuses on the reserve and
civilian population ages 19 to 30—and in some cases ages 19 to 24—with
a high school diploma.[1] We use several data sources, including the
Monitoring the Future (MtF) survey of high school seniors for various
years, the 1986, 1992, and 2000 Surveys of Reserve Component Personnel

_____
[1] We include GED holders in our definition of the population with a
high school diploma.

(RCS) provided to us by the Defense Manpower Data Center (DMDC), the March Current Population Survey (CPS) data for various years, and the 1979 and 1997 cohorts of the National Longitudinal Survey of Youth (NLSY). We find that while young reservists typically join the reserves with no more than a high school degree, they express a strong demand for higher education and a substantial fraction of reservists (23 percent, according to the 2000 RCS) do in fact obtain a college degree by age 30. Thus, like the overall population, the demand for college among reservists is high and has increased over time. We also find that the demand for college has increased throughout the AFQT distribution and, for men, especially among individuals scoring in Category II and below.

The nature of college attendance has changed over time, in part because college demand is rising among less skilled youth. We find that individuals in AFQT Categories I and II tend to pursue college much more intensively than those in Categories IIIA and IIIB. Less than one-third of Category III individuals finish a two- or four-year degree program within six years of their initial enrollment, and many of these individuals, no doubt, never finish. These individuals may have trouble completing their college studies because they must work intensively to finance their college education or, conversely, they work intensively because their returns upon receiving a college degree are relatively low.

To explore the relationship between work effort, enrollment intensity, and AFQT, we examined how reservists combine work and college. Reservists are particularly likely to work while attending college. Among reservists ages 19 to 24, 64 percent of those attending college reported working in a civilian job, compared to 52 percent of all civilian males in this age range attending college. Reservists also work more hours per week, conditional on working at all. We conducted regression analysis of the relationship between AFQT and work effort and college completion and find that the AFQT score has a negative effect on hours worked while in school and a positive effect on college-completion rates independent of family resources. This finding suggests that the latter explanation—those with lower AFQT work intensively because their returns to college are lower—may drive college completion rates in this population.

Consequently, while it is true that far more individuals desire a college education today than did 20 years ago, the kind of college experience the typical student demands has changed. The key populations the reserve components seek to recruit, those in Categories II-IIIB, have a higher propensity to attend college than in the past, as is well known. Less well known, however, is that this population typically attends college less intensively and completes college less rapidly than individuals in AFQT Category I. This latter observation suggests that educational benefits in the Reserves generally need not be tailored to individuals who pursue college intensively.

Are current educational benefits offered to reservists sufficient to meet recruiting goals? We provide a partial answer to this question by comparing educational benefits in the Reserves with other financial aid programs and by tabulating the level of satisfaction with these benefits among reservists. We find that 70 percent of reservists ages 19 to 30 enrolled in college are using military education benefits. Of these individuals, about 65 percent reported in the 2000 RCS that their education benefits were an important influence on their decision to stay in the Reserves. Furthermore, we find that the financial aid received by reservists ages 19 to 30 is comparable to aid received by civilians and military veterans. Reservists earn lower monthly financial aid benefits under their GI Bill than active duty members do under the MGIB, but reservists are not required to make contributions to their benefit nor wait to fulfill a service requirement before receiving the benefit. Accounting for these programmatic differences, we find that until recently, the present value of the GI Bill benefit for reservists exceeded the present value of the MGIB benefit. Furthermore, even in more recent years, whether present value of the reserve benefit exceeded the present value of active duty benefit depended on what assumption is made about members' personal discount rates. This comparison of the financial benefits did not account for the different demands of active duty and reserve service. Though reservists have been on call far more often and for longer durations since September 11, 2001, active duty members are on call every day and year round, frequently work long irregular hours, deploy more frequently, and are subject to frequent moves that are disruptive to family life. Thus, on the basis of these comparisons we conclude that existing educational benefit programs used by reservists are generally adequate in terms of reported satisfaction with these benefits and in terms of how they compare to benefits available to other populations.

POLICY DISCUSSION

Our descriptive analyses suggest that reserve service is generally compatible with college attendance and existing educational programs provide benefits that are comparable to those available to civilians and other military personnel. The risk of activation while in the Reserves, however, has increased over the past decade, especially in the aftermath of September 11, 2001. Activation disrupts schooling in a number of ways, and, although the U.S. Department of Defense (DoD), the U.S. Department of Education (DOEd), and the Department of Veterans' Affairs (DVA) have mechanisms and regulations to help reduce the financial loss associated with activation, many reservists report losses, and this risk of disruption and loss may be unacceptable to some potential recruits, especially those higher aptitude youth who wish to purse their college studies intensively and continuously. High-aptitude youth demand a college education and many of these individuals may demand a college experience that prohibits a risk of activation of uncertain duration.

To the extent that more AFQT Category I and II personnel are required in the reserve components across the board or in specific occupational areas, allowing some reservists to pursue college first without the risk of activation, and serve in the Reserves subsequently, might serve as an effective recruiting incentive. One possibility would be to create an ROTC-like program for enlisted personnel that would allow individuals to attend college at a two- or four-year institution while serving in a reserve unit but not be at risk for activation. Following their completion of college, they could be required to enlist for a longer term of service or perhaps serve with a higher risk of activation.

More formal analyses of these types of programs may be warranted in the future as the reserve components adjust to the demands of homeland security and the war on terrorism, international peacekeeping efforts, and the DoD's desire to more fully integrate the reserve and active duty forces. The 2002 Review of the Reserve Contributions to National Defense articulated a new vision of reserve service, known as a "Continuum of Service," which argues for more flexible management of reserve personnel and capabilities (Office of the Assistant Secretary of Defense for Reserve Affairs, 2002). An ROTC-like program for enlisted personnel of the sort described above is consistent with this new vision in that it recognizes that cost-effective personnel management may entail allowing some reservists to serve under enlistment contracts that are tailored to their particular needs and the needs of the reserve components.

Based on this preliminary assessment, we offer the following observations and recommendations with respect to restructuring education benefits in the Reserves:

- Reserve service is generally compatible with college attendance for the vast majority of reservists.
- Higher aptitude potential reserve recruits (those in AFQT Categories I and II) may perceive the potential disruption to their academic studies entailed by activation to be unacceptable.
- To the extent the reserve components seek to attract more high-aptitude recruits in the future, they may wish to experiment with recruiting programs that minimize the risk of activation while these individuals attend college.
- These programs should be targeted at high-aptitude recruits and recruits training in hard-to-fill reserve occupations; these programs must also offer greater protection from activation than is currently available to non-prior service recruits following their initial reserve training period.
- Implementation of these programs should entail an evaluation component similar in nature to the ongoing evaluation of the Army's College-First program.

ACKNOWLEDGMENTS

We would like to thank Mike Dove, Tim Elig, and Jim Caplan at the DMDC who provided data and documentation on the DMDC surveys of reserve personnel. We greatly appreciate the research assistance provided by Phoenix Do and Katya Fonkych at RAND and the comments of our RAND colleagues who attended our work-in-progress seminar. We are grateful for the input provided by Dr. Curt Gilroy, the Director of Accession Policy in the Office of the Under Secretary of Defense for Personnel and Readiness, and Major Tony Kanellis and Captain Derek Blough, both former staff members in the Office of Accession Policy. We also benefited from conversations with Mr. George Richon in the Office of Educational Services within the Veterans' Benefits Administration and Mr. Max Padilla, Project Director of the Service Members' Opportunity Colleges-National Guard. We also received valuable comments and assistance from Mr. Richard Krimmer, Director of Military Personnel Programs in the Office of the Assistant Secretary of Defense for Reserve Affairs, from Colonel Henry Payne formerly in that office, Captain Michael Price, and Lieutenant Colonel Henderson Baker. We received detailed comments from Bruce Orvis at RAND and Jennie Wegner at the Center for Naval Analyses, which were extremely helpful in producing this final report. Finally, we would like to thank Dr. John Winkler, the Deputy Assistant Secretary of Defense for Reserve Affairs (Manpower and Personnel) for his sponsorship of our project and his input to this research.

ABBREVIATIONS

Armed Forces Qualification Test	AFQT
Active Guard Reserve	AGR
Armed Services Vocational Aptitude Battery	ASVAB
College Assistance Student Head Start	CASH
Computer Adaptive Test version of the ASVAB	CAT-ASVAB
Current Population Survey	CPS
Defense Manpower Data Center	DMDC
Delayed Entry Program	DEP
Department of Veterans' Affairs	DVA
fiscal year (FY)	
Helping Outstanding Pupils Educationally program	HOPE
Loan Repayment Program	LRP
Monitoring the Future	MtF
Montgomery GI Bill	MGIB
Montgomery GI Bill-Selected Reserves	MGIB-SR
National Longitudinal Survey of Youth	NLSY
National Postsecondary Student Aid Study	NPSAS
Office of the Undersecretary of Defense for Personnel and Readiness	OSD-PR
present discounted value	PDV
Reserve Components Common Personnel Data System	RCCPDS
Reserve Component Personnel	RCP
Reserve Officer Training Corps	ROTC

Service Members' Opportunity Colleges	SOC
U.S. Department of Defense	DoD
U.S. Department of Education	DOEd

CHAPTER ONE INTRODUCTION

The contribution of the reserve components to the nation's defense has increased dramatically since the mid-1980s. Measured in terms of man-days, the Reserve components' contribution rose from an estimated 0.9 million in fiscal year (FY) 1986 to an estimated 12 million in FY 2000, and this contribution of man-days has continued to rise in the aftermath of September 11, 2001. During this time, the mission of the Reserves has changed considerably, becoming more diverse and integrated with the total force. Today, in addition to providing combat support to the active force, reservists participate in a wide range of civilian and military operations including peacekeeping, civil affairs, and homeland defense.

Overall, the number of recruits sought by the reserve components rose from about 141,800 in FY 1994 to 159,300 in FY 1999 and has since fallen to about 123,300 in FY 2004 (Figure 1.1). Despite an overall decline in the recruiting mission, the two largest reserve components, the Army Reserve and Army Guard, have increased their recruiting goals since 2001 (by about 8 percent for the Army Reserve and 7 percent for the Army Guard between 2001 and 2004). Looking to the future, a new defense strategy, one of transformation, has emerged where military planners emphasize developing capabilities to meet a spectrum of diverse and uncertain threats. As articulated by the Office of the Assistant Secretary of Defense for Reserve Affairs in its *Review of Reserve Component Contributions to National Defense* (2002), transformation will require a rebalancing of defense capabilities between the active and reserve forces as well as greater flexibility in how reserve personnel are accessed and managed. For example, rebalancing means military skills that are needed on a continuous basis would be concentrated in the active components while skills that are used more intermittently or are hard to retain, such as skills related to information technology, would be held in the reserve components. As such, the demand for high-quality personnel is likely to remain high in the Reserves for the foreseeable future.

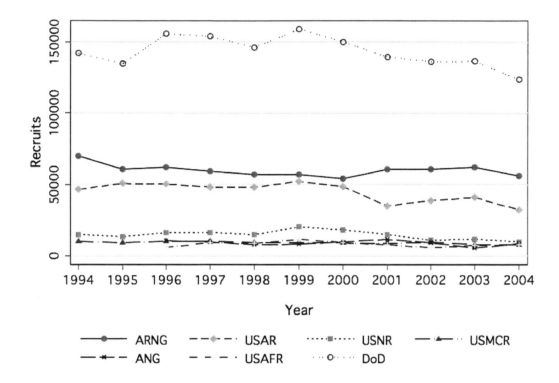

Figure 1.1 Reserve Components Total Recruiting Mission

SOURCE: Office of Accessions Policy, Office of the Secretary of Defense.

The enlistment of high-quality recruits, where high-quality is defined as having a high school diploma and scoring in the top half of the distribution of the Armed Forces Qualification Test (AFQT) (Categories I-IIIA), has long been the primary mission of military recruiters in both the active and reserve forces. In the active force, the services expect at least 90 percent of their accessions to have a high school diploma and at least 60 percent to score in AFQT Categories I-IIIA. While the active components generally saw the fraction of their total accessions considered high quality decline during the 1990s, high-quality, non-prior service accessions in the Reserves remained relatively constant. Since the mid-1990s, the percentage of non-prior service reserve recruits possessing a high school diploma has held steady at slightly below 90 percent, while the percentage scoring in AFQT Categories I-IIIA has averaged about 66 percent since 1998 (see Figure 1.2). Some reserve components, most notably the Army and Naval

- 3 -

Reserve, missed their prior service recruiting mission in 2000 by a substantial margin (10 and 35 percent, respectively). In 2001, all components met their non-prior service accession mission, while the Air Guard, Army National Guard, and Army Reserve missed their prior service recruiting mission. Consequently, the Air National Guard missed its overall accession goal in 2001. In 2002, the Naval Reserve and Air Force Reserve both missed their prior service accession mission. They exceeded their non-prior service mission, however, and ultimately exceeded their total recruiting mission. In 2003, all components, with the exception of the Army Guard, met their total accession mission. In 2004, both the Army and National Guard failed to meet their total accession missions.[2]

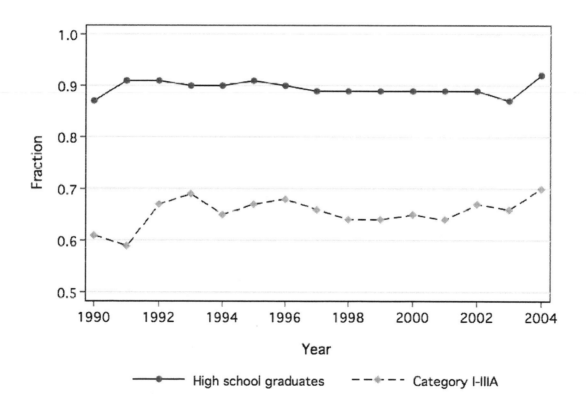

Figure 1.2 Fraction of Non-Prior Service Reserve Accessions with High-School Diplomas and Scoring in AFQT Categories I-IIIA

SOURCE: Office of Accessions Policy, Office of the Secretary of Defense.

_____

[2] The Office of Accession Policy within the Office of the Under Secretary of Defense provided these figures for Personnel and Readiness.

A tightening labor market coupled with perceived hardships associated with recent reserve activations may result in recruiting shortfalls in coming years. A potential difficulty for reserve recruiting—and the focus of this study—is the continued rise in the rate of college enrollment among high school graduates. The fraction of high school graduates who enroll in postsecondary education institutions within two years of graduation rose from about half in 1980 to about two-thirds in 1999 (U.S. Bureau of the Census, 2002) and it is clear that the vast majority of American youth now expect to obtain some postsecondary education during their lifetime. Several recent studies have investigated how rising college enrollment could affect recruiting in the active forces, but we are aware of only one study focusing explicitly on how the college market impacts reserve recruiting.[3]

Studies of active force recruiting and the college market find that high-quality youth treat military service as a substitute for college attendance, not as a complement. Warner, Simon, and Payne (2001), for example, find that a 10 percent increase in college enrollment reduces high-quality enlistments in the Army by an estimated 10 percent (i.e., an estimated elasticity of Army enlistment with respect to college enrollment of -1.0). Direct qualitative survey data also supports the contention that high-quality youth perceive college enrollment and military enlistment as substitutes for each other. When asked why they planned not to enlist in the military, half of respondents to a 2000 survey of college-bound youth and young adults already in college stated that military service would interfere with their educational plans (Asch, Schonlau, and Du, 2003). Thus, postsecondary colleges and

---

[3] Studies of reserve accessions include Tan (1991), who studied non- prior-service accessions and Marquis and Kirby (1989), who analyzed prior-service accessions. Kostiuk and Grogan (1987) and Shiells (1986) studied Naval Reserve accessions. While these studies provide information on the effects of recruiters and other factors on reserve enlistments, they do not address the implications of rising college enrollment and the effects of reserve education benefits on reserve accessions. Arkes and Kilburn (2002), which we discuss later in this section, empirically test for the effect of state-level education benefits (both from the National Guard and other state sources) on reserve accessions.

universities compete directly with the military for high-quality youth, and this competition is likely to intensify as college expectations continue to rise.

The effect of heightened college demand on reserve recruiting is likely to differ from that on active force recruiting for a number of reasons. First, when not activated, reservists can attend college while they fulfill their reserve obligation of one weekend a month and two weeks per year. Second, the reserve components offer an array of educational opportunities to individuals who wish to attend college while serving in the Reserves. For example, most reservists qualify for the Montgomery GI Bill-Selected Reserves (MGIB-SR) program and some members of the National Guard components are entitled to state-funded college tuition breaks and grants. Additionally, many reservists qualify for loan repayment programs and some receive additional funds if they serve in highly demanded military occupations. Third, prior service members make up about 45 percent of total reserve accessions, and it is not clear that these prior service recruits will treat college and military service in the same manner as non-prior service recruits, who are typically much younger.

Consequently, whether potential reserve recruits think of college and reserve service as substitutes is unclear. On the one hand, reserve service is generally part-time and the majority of college students today work while attending college. In this sense, reserve service, like part-time work, may facilitate college attendance and so be complementary. On the other hand, some potential reserve recruits may wish to pursue college more intensively than is permitted by a reserve career, especially if one considers the risk that activation could seriously interrupt college studies. More generally, existing programs that offer educational opportunities in the Reserves may not fit well with the educational and career aspirations of college-bound youth. For these individuals, reserve service and college attendance may not be so complementary.

The only empirical evidence on this question of complementarity or substitutability of reserve service and college attendance comes from a recent study by Arkes and Kilburn (2002), who model the propensity to

enlist in the Reserves as a function of recruiting resources,
demographic variables, labor market conditions, and educational
benefits. The authors find that reserve recruiting lags in states that
offer merit-based scholarships, like Georgia's "Helping Outstanding
Pupils Educationally" (HOPE) program, which supports the hypothesis that
reserve service and college attendance are substitutes. The authors also
find, however, that states with relatively high tuition rates have
relatively low rates of reserve enlistment. Curiously, state tuition
rates were found to be positively correlated with active duty
enlistments. It may be then that youth living in states with high
tuition rates prefer to join the active duty force and gain access to
MGIB benefits rather than join the Reserves, whose educational benefits
are much smaller (at least in nominal terms—see below for more on this
subject).

Under the assumption that most college-bound youth view service and
college attendance as substitutes, the active duty components have
enhanced their major college benefit programs in recent years in an
effort to attract more high-quality recruits. Some programs allow
enlistees to accrue college funds for use after separating from the
military, while other programs provide tuition assistance and distance-
learning opportunities for enlistees interested and able to begin
college while still serving. However, many potential recruits want to
begin their college studies immediately after completing high school,
and some components have recently responded to that demand by offering
new programs in which enlistees pursue college first and military
service second. For example, the Army's "College-First" program allows
recruits to attend college for up to two years and then enter the
military at a higher pay grade. The Navy's "Tech-Prep" program allows
individuals to attend college in a military-related skill area, such as
medical technology, and subsequently enter the Navy in that particular
skill area. These new programs seek to make college enrollment and
military service more complementary and attract individuals who prefer
to complete their military obligation after beginning their
postsecondary studies. The Navy's Tech-Prep program has not been
formally evaluated. As we describe in greater detail in the final

section of this report, the College-First program has demonstrated that offering the option to begin college before active duty enlistment is attractive to some college-bound youth and measurably increased enlistment rates in affected recruiting districts (Orvis, 2001).

Currently, there are no educational benefit programs that offer reservists the opportunity to attend college with military financing prior to assuming the full responsibilities of affiliating with a reserve unit, and it is possible that the lack of such opportunities deters some potential recruits from enlisting. The RAND Corporation was asked to provide a preliminary evaluation of whether programs similar in nature to the Army's College-First program or the Navy's Tech-Prep program could enhance the ability of the reserve components to attract and retain high-quality non-prior and prior service recruits and whether the potential of these programs warrants a more systematic and extensive evaluation, including randomized field trials.

Because we could not specifically test the hypothesis that restructured educational benefits enhance reserve recruiting, we instead took a more qualitative and descriptive approach to this preliminary evaluation. We began by reexamining how changes in the demand for college among youth in general, and reservists in particular, impacts the ability of the Reserves to attract high-quality youth. We paid special attention to how the heightened demand for college has changed the composition of those who now attend college. The results of this reexamination can be found in Chapter 2. We then sought to describe how reservists currently combine their reserve service with civilian employment and college attendance. We also asked how the changing composition of the college market has affected the intensity with which typical college students pursue their postsecondary studies. Chapter 3 summarizes these results. Reservists are currently entitled to a wide range of educational benefits. We cataloged these benefits and considered how these benefits compare to educational benefits available to civilians and active duty veterans. These comparisons are presented in Chapter 4.

After synthesizing these descriptive analyses of the significance of the college market, how reservists and civilians combine work and

schooling, and the educational benefits currently available to
reservists, we then considered whether restructured educational benefits
are likely to affect the reserve enlistment decision of high-quality
youth and, if so, which types of potential recruits would be affected.
Chapter 5 presents our conclusions from this synthesis.

We note here that the Reserves are comprised of two different
groups of individuals: those with no prior military service and those
with prior military service. Non-prior service recruits accounted for 55
percent of total reserve accessions in 2003 with the fraction varying
from 75 percent in the Marine Corps Reserve to 40 percent in the Air
Guard and Naval Reserve. For the most part, we do not explicitly
distinguish between prior and non-prior service recruits in this report,
although many of our tabulations are conducted by age (ages 19 to 24 and
25 to 30). Younger reservists are more likely to be non-prior service.
The analyses we present below, however, are perhaps most relevant to the
problem of attracting and retaining younger non-prior service recruits.
Prior service recruits typically have access to more substantial
educational benefits they earned as members of the active duty force and
will not use existing educational benefits available to them through the
Reserves. Non-prior service recruits also typically have lower levels of
education when they enlist in the Reserves and so may want the Reserves
to finance more years of education than prior service recruits, who may
already have obtained some higher education while on active duty. Both
prior and non-prior service recruits, however, face the risk of
activation while attending school, so new educational benefits that aim
to minimize schooling disruptions attributable to activation could be
desirable from the perspective of either group.

Our descriptive analyses are derived from a range of data sources,
which we describe in a Data Appendix (Appendix A) that can be found at
the end of this report. These data sets include various years of the
Annual March Demographic Supplement to the Current Population Survey
(CPS), the 1979 and 1997 cohorts of the National Longitudinal Surveys of
Youth (NLSY), the 2000 National Postsecondary Student Aid Study (NPSAS),
the September 1999 extract of the Reserve Components Common Personnel
Data System (RRCPDS), and the 1986, 1992, and 2000 Surveys of Reserve

Component Personnel (RCS). Beyond providing basic information about these surveys, the Data Appendix explains sample restrictions and reports sample sizes. Where appropriate, some of this information is provided in the main body of the report as well.

CHAPTER TWO THE COLLEGE MARKET

For obvious reasons, appealing to America's youth has long been at the heart of military recruiting. The Reserves, like the active duty forces, draw the vast majority of their new recruits from the population ages 29 and younger. In 1999, 50 percent of new prior service and 84 percent of new non-prior service recruits were ages 25 and younger.[4] Non-prior service recruits, who accounted for 67 percent of all recent recruits ages 19 to 30 in that year, are even younger; indeed, more than 40 percent of non-prior service recruits were 18 years and younger and three-quarters were ages 22 and younger (see Figure 2.1). Not long ago, the U.S. military's primary competitors in the labor market were civilian employers seeking to hire high school graduates. Today, the nation's two- and four-year colleges and universities compete at least as strongly as civilian employers for high school graduates, a fact that is well known among military recruiters and personnel managers. Targeting the so-called college market is now a principle recruiting objective in both the reserve and active duty forces.

In this section, we first present evidence that the demand for a college education has risen strongly among America's youth in general and, more specifically, among reservists themselves. We then examine the AFQT distribution of the college-bound population and how that has changed over time. The Reserves, like the Active Duty forces, draws the bulk of its enlistees from Categories IIIA and IIIB, and we argue here and in later sections that it is the demand for college among this population of youth that the Reserves most needs to address with its educational benefits.

In this and other sections to follow, we focus on the population ages 19 to 30 with a high school degree.[5] In some instances, we restrict

---

[4] We define a recent recruit as a reservist who first enters reserve service within 12 months of the survey date (September 1999).

[5] We note here that the composition of high school graduates has changed over time. CPS data indicate that 80.3 percent of 18-24 year-olds held a regular high school diploma and 4.2 percent held a GED or other equivalency degree in 1988 (the first year the CPS collected such

our tabulations to males because males dominate the reserve forces. When referring to reservists, we mean enlisted reservists.

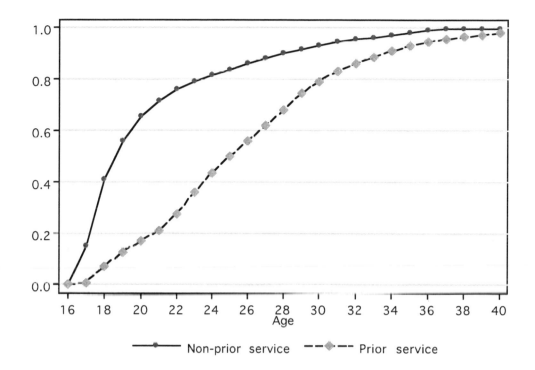

Figure 2.1 Cumulative Percent Age Distribution of Recent Reserve Enlisted Recruits: 1999

Notes: Recent recruits are defined as those reservists entering reserve service for the first time within one year of the survey date. Sample is restricted to selected reservists.
SOURCE: 1999 RCCPDS.

2.1 RISING EXPECTATIONS AND COLLEGE ATTENDANCE

The Monitoring the Future (MTF) Study each year asks high school seniors whether they expect to eventually graduate from a two- or four-year college. In 2001, 58 percent of high school seniors stated they definitely will graduate from a four-year college and 22 percent said they probably would. The percentage stating they definitely or probably

data). In 1999, 76.8 percent held a regular high school diploma and 9.2 percent held a GED or other equivalency degree. Thus, the relative supply of traditional high school graduates, which the Services prefer, has declined.

will graduate from a two-year college was 19 and 22 percent in 2001. In Figure 2.2, we see that the percentages reporting they definitely will graduate from a two- or four-year college have increased considerably in a short period of time. In 1980, 35 percent of high school seniors said they would definitely graduate from a four-year college and 12 percent said they would definitely graduate from a two-year college. The increase in educational expectations has been substantial for both males and females. In 1980, 36 percent of males and 34 percent of females reported they expected they definitely would graduate from a four-year college. By 2001, these percentages were 51 and 63 percent, respectively.

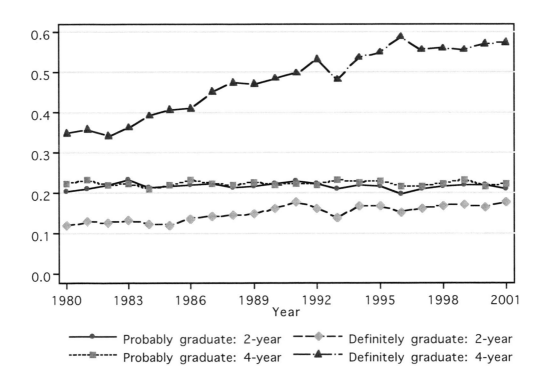

Figure 2.2 College Expectations of High School Seniors in Percent: 1980-2001

Notes: Sample restricted to high school seniors reporting that they expect to graduate in June.
SOURCE: 1980-2001 MTF.

For males especially, college enrollment and completion rates have not risen as sharply as have college expectations. Data from the March CPS show that, for males, college enrollment among individuals ages 19 to 24 increased only slightly (from 34 to 39 percent)[6] while the percentage of individuals ages 25 to 30 with a college degree remained almost constant (Figure 2.3).[7] The percentage of males with some college declined in the 1980s, but by 2001 it had returned to its 1980 level. For females, on the other hand, college enrollment and completion rates have tracked rising college expectations more closely (see Figure 2.4). In 1980, 53 percent of females ages 25 to 30 reported having completed some college (one or more years of college) and 24 percent reported having completed four or more years of college. By 2001, these figures had increased to 69 and 34 percent, respectively. In 2001, 64 percent of females who were between the ages of 19 and 24 reported having completed some college, up from 52 percent in 1980. Current college enrollment among females ages 19 to 24 increased from 29 to 40 percent between 1986 and 2001.

---

[6] In the March CPS, current college enrollment can only be determined after 1986 and for individuals who are ages 24 and younger.

[7] The CPS changed how it measures educational attainment in 1992. Prior to 1992, the CPS asked respondents to report highest grade completed. Starting in 1992, the CPS asked respondents to report highest degree completed. We assume individuals who report 16 or more years of completed education prior to 1992 would have reported having had completed a bachelor's degree had they instead been asked to report highest degree completed.

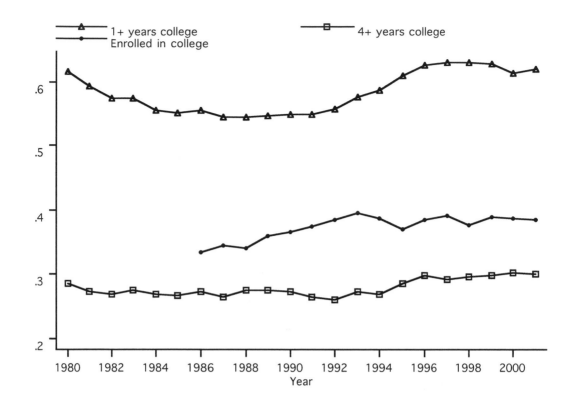

Figure 2.3 Male Educational Attainment (Ages 25 to 30) and College Enrollment (Ages 19 to 24): 1980-2001

Notes: Sample restricted to males with at least 12 years of education.
SOURCE: 1988-2001 March CPS.

Since the Reserves, like the Active force, are largely comprised of males, it is tempting to conclude that the aggregate rise in college attendance poses little problem for the Reserves, because increasing college attendance among females, not males, has been the driving trend. But there are at least three reasons why this conclusion may be premature. First, women comprise a growing fraction of the Reserve forces. According to the RCCPDS, the percentage of reservists who are female increased from 13 to 17 percent between 1987 and 1999, and, in 1999, 24 percent of recently recruited reservists were female. As barriers to female participation in the reserves fall, the importance of attracting the college market will grow. Second, college expectations have risen considerably for both males and females. While youth expectations are not always realized, they strongly influence the choices young men and women make and how they perceive the relative benefits of the various educational and work-related options open to them.

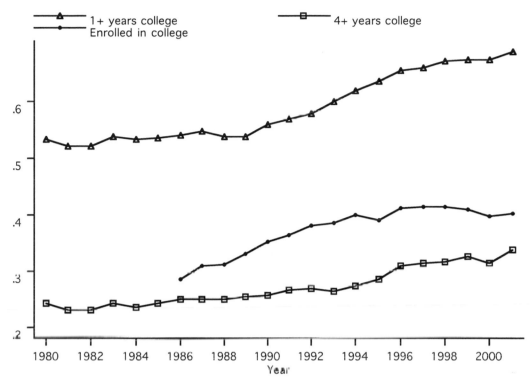

Figure 2.4 Female Educational Attainment (Ages 25 to 30) and College Enrollment (Ages 19 to 24): 1980-2001

Note: Sample restricted to females with at least 12 years of education. SOURCE: 1988-2001 March CPS.

Finally, we have seen substantial increases in the demand for college among both male and female reservists. The vast majority of reservists begin their reserve service, regardless of prior service status, with no more than a high school degree. In 1999, 83 percent of first-year prior service reservists entered with a high school level education. A substantial percentage of first-year non-prior service reservists (37 percent) have yet to even complete a high school degree when they first begin to drill with a reserve unit; and 53 percent have a high school level education. Nonetheless, most reservists expect to eventually earn a baccalaureate degree or better. According to the 2000 RCS, 77 percent of reservists ages 19 to 24 expect to eventually earn at least a bachelors degree. In contrast, in 1986, fewer than half of all surveyed reservists expected to earn a baccalaureate degree (see Table 2.1).

In Table 2.1, we see that the educational attainment of reservists has increased along with expectations.[8] The percentage of reservists ages 25 to 30 with at least some college increased sharply between 1986 and 2000, from 21 to 34 percent. The percentage of these reservists completing an associates degree increased from 10 to 18 percent and the percentage completing a baccalaureate degree increased from 10 to 23 percent. Much of this increase in educational attainment occurred between 1986 and 1992. Although these statistics indicate that reservists attained somewhat less education by ages 25 to 30 than the overall population,[9] the statistics nonetheless reflect a strong and increasing interest in higher education among this population. In 2000, 20 percent of reservists ages 19 to 24 were enrolled in a two-year degree program and 34 percent were currently enrolled in a four-year degree program. This rate of college enrollment is substantially higher than the rate of college enrollment reported in the CPS for males ages 19 to 24 with at least a high school degree in 2000 (39 percent overall).

---

[8] We report figures for both male and female reservists here. Females represent about 18 percent of the total RCS sample and their inclusion does not have a substantial impact on the means we report in Table 2.1.

[9] CPS data treat individuals who have completed less than one year of college as having some college. The RCS data classify these individuals as having no college.

Table 2.1

**Educational Expectations, Attainment, and Enrollment Among Reservists
Ages 19 to 30: 1986, 1992, 2000**

	1986	1992	2000
Ages 19-24			
Expect to Receive			
Associates Degree	0.13	0.15	0.13
Bachelors Degree	0.47	0.70	0.77
Educational Attainment			
Some College	0.28	0.46	0.43
Associates Degree	0.05	0.13	0.09
Bachelors Degree	0.03	0.07	0.07
Current Enrollment			
2-Year	0.10	0.18	0.20
4-Year	0.22	0.36	0.34
Ages 25-30			
Expect to Receive			
Associates Degree	0.15	0.18	0.16
Bachelors Degree	0.45	0.60	0.73
Educational Attainment			
Some College	0.21	0.35	0.34
Associates Degree	0.10	0.15	0.18
Bachelors Degree	0.10	0.16	0.23
Current Enrollment			
2-Year	0.08	0.12	0.13
4-Year	0.13	0.22	0.24

Note: See Appendix A for sample definition.
SOURCE: 1986, 1992, and 2000 RCS

The apparent rise in the demand for college among young Americans is most sensibly attributable to a perception that the financial returns to attaining a college degree have risen. The popular press and media certainly feed this perception. Whether or not the financial returns to college have in fact increased is not entirely clear: Determining the causal effect of education on labor market earnings is notoriously difficult due to the likely strong correlation between innate ability, labor market prospects, and educational attainment (e.g., Card, 2000). Nonetheless, it is abundantly clear that the labor market earnings of the college educated relative to the non-college educated rose rapidly over the 1980s and 1990s.[10] This is true for both men and women, although the relative returns to education rose somewhat more rapidly for men. Normalizing weekly earnings to an indexed value of one in 1980, we see in Figure 2.5 that the real weekly wages of college graduates rose 20 percent between 1980 and 2000; the real weekly wages of high school graduates, by comparison, were roughly constant over that period.

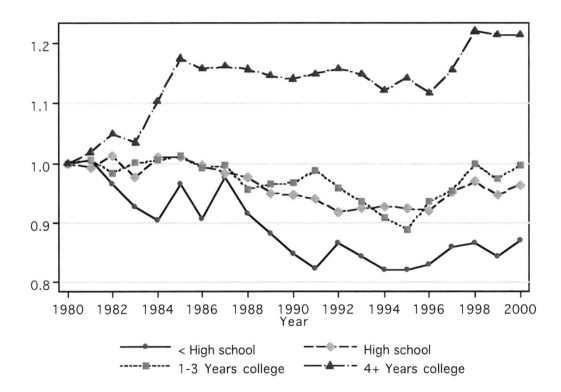

Figure 2.5 Growth in Real Weekly Wages Among Individuals Ages 26 to 31: 1980-2000
Notes: Sample restricted to individuals ages 26 to 31 reporting positive labor earnings, weeks and hours worked in the preceding calendar year. Weekly wages are deflated by the CPI (1982 = 100) and normalized to one in 1980.
SOURCE: 1980-2001 March CPS.

---

[10] What has caused the relative wages of college-educated individuals to rise in recent decades is not well understood. Some have argued that recent technological advances favor more educated workers or workers with higher cognitive ability (Juhn, Murphy, and Pierce, 1993), while others argue trade and institutional changes are responsible (DiNardo, Fortin, and Lemieux, 1996) and others argue that the relative supply of college-educated workers has declined (Card and DiNardo, 2002; Card and Lemieux, 2000).

2.2 THE AFQT COMPOSITION OF COLLEGE-BOUND YOUTH

As the demand for college increases, the composition of the
college-bound population may change as well. In this section we focus on
cognitive ability as measured by scores on the Armed Services Vocational
Aptitude Battery (ASVAB). The Reserves, like the active duty forces,
requires its non-prior service enlisted recruits to obtain a minimum
score on the ASVAB.[11] The ASVAB consists of a sequence of tests that
measure knowledge and skill in the following ten areas: general science;
arithmetic reasoning; word knowledge; paragraph comprehension; numerical
operations; coding speed; auto and shop information; mathematics
knowledge; mechanical comprehension; and electronic information. DoD
derives the AFQT score from a subset of the ASVAB—word knowledge,
paragraph comprehension, math knowledge, and arithmetic reasoning.
Currently, DoD categorizes potential recruits according to eight AFQT
categories: Categories V, IVC, IVB, IVA, IIIB, IIIA, II, and I
corresponding to the 9th, 15th, 20th, 30th, 49th, 64th, and 92nd
percentiles of a nationally-normed AFQT distribution, respectively.

In 1999, four percent of enlisted first-year, non-prior service
reserve recruits scored above the 92nd percentile (Category I), 31
percent between the 65th and 92nd percentiles (Category II), 23 percent
between the 50th and 64th percentiles (Category IIIA), and 40 percent
between the 31st and 49th percentiles (Category IIIB) (see Table 2.2).
Only two percent came from Category IV; by law, the Reserves may not
enlist more than 20 percent of its accessions from Category IV, and
Category V individuals are not eligible to enlist. First-year, prior
service recruits joined the Reserves with somewhat higher AFQT scores,
which is expected, since promotion is positively correlated with AFQT.
More than half of all new reservists, then, come from between the 31st
and 64th percentiles of the AFQT distribution.

---

[11] Each service has its own regulations with respect to minimum
education and AFQT requirements. For high school graduates, minimum AFQT
scores are 16, 40, 31, and 21 for the Army, Air Force, Navy, and Marine
Corps, respectively. Individuals with less than a high school degree
(including GED holders) face stricter AFQT requirements.

Table 2.2

Distribution of New Reserve Recruits by AFQT Category

AFQT Category	Non-Prior Service	Prior Service
I	0.04	0.06
II	0.31	0.42
IIIA	0.23	0.28
IIIB	0.40	0.22
IV & V[a]	0.02	0.02

Note: Sample restricted to selected enlisted reservists entering reserve service for the first time within one year of survey date.
[a]Reporting error may account for the presence of Category V recruits in the RCCPDS.
SOURCE: September 1999 RCCPDS.

We employ the 1979 and 1997 cohorts of the NLSY to examine how college expectations and attendance have changed over time within the AFQT distribution. The current norms for the AFQT are derived from the 1979 cohort and the 1997 cohort will serve as the basis for a new AFQT norm beginning July 2004. Because the official DoD norm using the 1997 cohort was not available at the time of our study, and because the 1979 and 1997 cohort ASVAB raw scores are not directly comparable, we construct our own AFQT distributions for 1979 and 1997 using the following approach.[12] First, we restrict our sample to the NLSY population ages 19 to 21 in 1983 and 2001. The year 2001 is the last survey year for which data is available from the NLSY97. These survey respondents were ages 14 to 17 when they took the ASVAB in 1980 or 1997/98. We then perform a principal components analysis on the four components of the ASVAB that DoD uses to derive the AFQT.[13] Principal components analysis transforms a number of typically correlated

---

[12] The 1997 NLSY cohort was administered using a Computer Adaptive Test version of the ASVAB (CAT-ASVAB). The sequence of questions asked by the CAT-ASVAB depends on prior answers. The raw scores from the CAT-ASVAB cannot be directly compared to the pencil-and-paper version of the test administered to the 1979 NLSY cohort.

[13] Because age in our samples ranges from 14 to 17, we first adjust each of the four component ASVAB scores for age by regressing each component score on an intercept and a quartic in age in months and taking the residual score.

variables into a smaller number of uncorrelated variables, called principal components, while maintaining the variability in the original variables. More specifically, a principal component is a linear combination of the original standardized ($\mu = 0, \sigma = 1$) variables (in this case, the four ASVAB components listed above) that maximizes the variance of that combination and has a zero covariance with all prior principal components. We take the first principal component as our measure of AFQT. We then weight the first principal component using the NLSY79 and NLSY97 sampling weights to arrive at a nationally normed AFQT index for each cohort.[14]

Our derived AFQT index simply marks the relative position of individuals within the AFQT distribution as measured in 1979 and 1997. For example, Category II in 1979 denotes individuals who score between the 64th and 92nd percentiles of the 1979 AFQT distribution. Similarly, Category II in 1997 denotes individuals who score between the 64th and 92nd percentiles of the 1997 AFQT distribution. Thus, when we make statements about how the propensity of Category II individuals to attend college has changed over time, we are simply computing how the propensity to attend college has changed for individuals who score in the same relative part of the overall AFQT distribution.[15]

------

[14] For the 1979 cohort, we can compare our derived AFQT index with the official normed AFQT percentile score. Our derived measure categorizes individuals in the same AFQT Category as the official normed score in 62 percent of cases. The mean absolute difference between the two measures is 3 percentile points. We suspect the difference arises because we restrict our sample to a younger group than that used to derive the overall AFQT norms. The AFQT norms were based on individuals ages 17 to 23. Our sample was between ages 14 and 17 at the time they were administered the exam.

[15] As noted in the text above, DoD will release revised AFQT norms in July 2004. The renorming will account for secular changes in scores on specific ASVAB components (specifically, increases in math and verbal scores and decreases in technical scores) (Segall 2003). While our exact approach to developing consistent AFQT scales across cohorts is different from that used by DoD in the renorming, the basic idea is the same, which is for an individual's AFQT score to reflect his or her position in the overall AFQT distribution for his or her cohort (i.e., a score of 50 means an individual scored in the 50th percentile of his or her cohort). As such, AFQT renorming should have no impact on the conclusions we draw below.

It is well known that AFQT scores are positively correlated with college enrollment (see, for example, MaCurdy and Vytlacil, 2002; Neal and Johnson, 1996). This correlation is evident in Figure 2.6, which shows the fraction of NLSY respondents ages 19 to 21 reporting they have attended at least one year of college by AFQT category. Looking at the 1997 cohort, the fraction of males with some college rises from 6 percent among individuals in Category V to 84 percent among individuals in Category I. We also see in Figure 2.6 that the fraction of youth reporting they attended at least one year of college increased somewhat for males and strongly for females across almost the entire AFQT distribution between 1979 and 1997. For males, the largest increases in the fraction with some college was among individuals scoring in Categories II, IVA, and IVC, whereas, for females, the fraction with some college increased sharply across the entire AFQT distribution. A similar pattern is evident if we look at the change in the fraction that ever enrolled in college by ages 19 to 21 (Figure 2.7).

We see even larger increases between the 1979 and 1997 cohorts in the fraction who report they expect to complete at least 16 years of education (Figure 2.8). For males, the largest increases in expectations are for those individuals scoring in Categories II, IIIA, and IVC, while, for females, large increases in expectations were registered for all but individuals scoring in Category V.

Based on the results in Figures 2.6 and 2.7, it would appear that the composition of the college-bound population, and conversely, the non-college-bound population has changed relatively little. In other words, in 1979 the population of youth who had ever attended college by age 19 to 21 looked quite similar in terms of AFQT scores to the same population of youth in 1997. For both males and females, though, the large increases in the fraction of youth who expected to complete at least 16 years of education has led to some small changes in composition. In 1979, 37 percent of males and 39 percent of females who did not expect to obtain a college degree scored above the 49th percentile of the AFQT distribution; in 1997, 31 and 36 percent of these males and females scored above the 49th percentile.

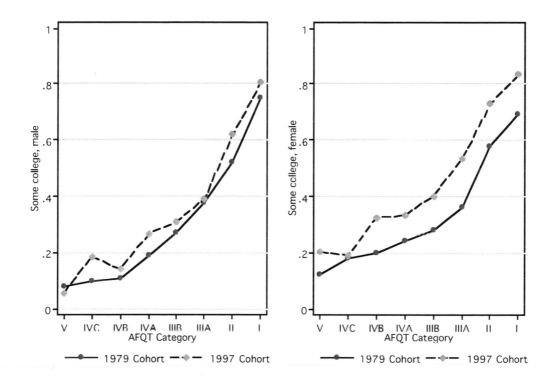

Figure 2.6 Fraction of Youth with Some College by AFQT Category and Cohort

Notes: Sample restricted to individuals ages 19 to 21 with a high school degree in 1983 and 2001. See text for derivation of AFQT categories. SOURCE: 1979 and 1997 NLSY.

- 24 -

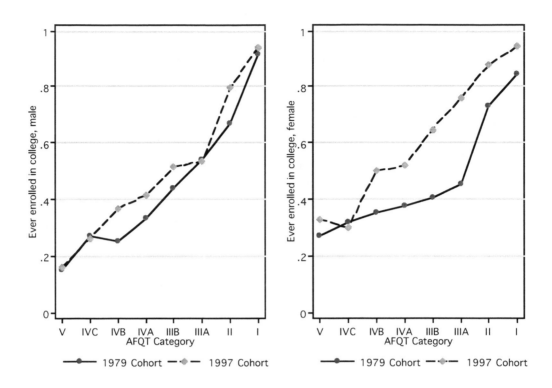

Figure 2.7 Fraction of Youth Ever Enrolled by AFQT Category and Cohort

Notes: Sample restricted to individuals ages 19 to 21 with a high school
degree in 1983 and 2001. See text for derivation of AFQT categories.
SOURCE: 1979 and 1997 NLSY.

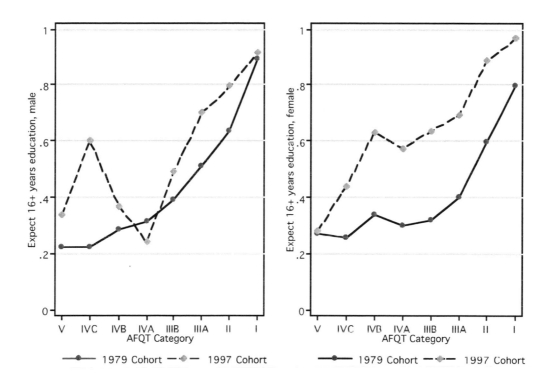

Figure 2.8 Fraction of Youth Expecting to Complete 16 or More Years of Education by AFQT Category and Cohort

Notes: Sample restricted to individuals ages 19 to 21 with a high school degree in 1983 and 2001. See text for derivation of AFQT categories.
SOURCE: 1979 and 1997 NLSY.

2.3 SUMMARY

The vast majority of reservists are in their early- to mid-20s when they first join a reserve component. The data show that while these individuals typically join the Reserves with no more than a high school degree, they express a strong demand for higher education and a substantial fraction of reservists (23 percent, according to the 2000 RCS) do in fact obtain a college degree by age 30. While the rate of college attendance has remained fairly constant for males overall since 1980, educational attainment among males who join the Reserves has increased considerably. Educational attainment has risen strongly among both civilian females and females who participate in the Reserves.

Survey data indicate that most youth today expect to obtain a two- or four-year college degree. That these rising expectations are not realized for a growing fraction of youth, especially males, suggests that the composition of those who go to college is changing. We showed in this section, however, that the overall AFQT distribution of college-bound youth did not change appreciably between the 1979 and 1997 NLSY cohorts. In the next section, we examine how the nature of college attendance has changed over time and, importantly, how it varies across the AFQT distribution.

CHAPTER THREE THE CHANGING NATURE OF COLLEGE ATTENDANCE

Working while attending college is common, perhaps more so today than ever. We show in this section that reservists are particularly likely to work while in college, and we argue that this behavior is most plausibly related to the types of individuals the Reserves tend to recruit. That is, the Reserves recruit individuals with a strong demand to attend college, but not necessarily a strong demand to complete a college program in an intensive fashion. This observation is important when considering whether current educational benefits are properly structured to appeal to the college demands of likely reserve recruits.

3.1 COMBINING WORK AND COLLEGE IN THE RESERVES

Survey responses from the 2000 RCS indicate that the structure of reserve duty permits continuous civilian employment: 84 percent of enlisted male reservists ages 19 to 30 reported working in the civilian sector in 2000. This figure is comparable to the overall level of employment among all civilian males of that age with at least a high school degree (78 percent in 2000). Remarkably, 67 percent of male reservists ages 19 to 30 attending a two- or four-year college degree program also reported working in a civilian occupation, and 64 percent of male reservists attending college ages 19 to 24 reported working in a civilian occupation. By comparison, only 52 percent of civilian males ages 19 to 24 worked while attending a two or four-year college program in 2000.[16]

Work hours per week are reported for the past calendar year only in the reserve surveys and, unfortunately, we cannot determine school attendance in the prior year. Thus, in Table 3.1 we compare hours per week and weeks worked per year in the past calendar year for male reservists and civilians who reported attending school in the reserve surveys. Reservists attending school devote a substantial number of hours per week to their civilian jobs. Conditional on working at all,

---

[16] We can determine current school enrollment in the March CPS for individuals ages 24 and under only.

the average reservist between the ages of 19 and 24 who attends school
worked 36 hours per week and 37 weeks per year;[17] 55 percent of these
reservists worked at least 40 hours per week. These figures compare to
30 hours per week and 32 weeks per year among all civilian males between
the ages 19 and 24 who attend school, with 31 percent working at least
40 hours per week. Note that these labor supply figures reported in the
2000 RCS do not include reserve service, which adds a minimum of 16
hours per month, plus 80 hours per year. When we include the minimum
amount of reserve service, we find that the mean number of weeks per
year increases to approximately 39 weeks among working reservists
attending school. The figures are somewhat higher for reservists ages 25
to 30. For example, 76 percent of reservists ages 25 to 30 enrolled in
college are also employed.

Table 3.1

Labor Supply of Males Currently Enrolled in College

	Reservists			Civilians
	19-24	25-30		19-24
Currently employed (2000)	0.64	0.76		0.52
Hours/week last calendar year (2000)	36	42		30
Weeks/year last calendar year (1986)				
Civilian	37	42		32
Civilian + Regular Reserve Duty	39	44		—
≥40 Hours/week (2000)	55	79		31

Notes: Sample restricted to males reporting being currently
enrolled in college. Hours per week and weeks per year are
reported for the last calendar year.
SOURCES: 1986 and 2000 RCS, and the 1986 and 2000 March CPS.

In Figure 3.1, we track current employment and mean hours worked in
the pervious week for civilian males ages 19 to 24 attending school
between 1987 and 2002. The figure shows a general increase in the

---

[17] Weeks per year last calendar year are reported for 1986 because
the 1992 and 2000 RCS did not collect this information. Between 1986 and
2000, average weeks per year increased from 32 to 36 for civilians age
19 to 24 enrolled in school.

fraction of individuals in school who also work and a slight increase in hours worked in the previous week. RCS data indicate a slight increase in employment among reservists ages 19 to 24 attending school between 1986 and 2000, from 58 to 64 percent (not shown in Figure 3.1). Next, we argue that this trend could reflect the increase in college demand among lower AFQT individuals.

Figure 3.1 Employment and Hours of Work for Currently Enrolled Males Ages 19 to 24: 1986-2001

Notes: Samples restricted to males ages 19 to 24 with at least a high school degree currently attending college.
SOURCES: 1986, 1992, and 2000 RCS; 1986-2001 March CPS.

3.2 WHO WORKS WHILE ATTENDING COLLEGE?

While a large fraction of college students are employed while attending school, work intensity varies considerably and, as we show in Tables 3.2-3.4, is correlated with ability. This correlation could arise for a variety of reasons. First, the most able students may have the most to gain by completing a college degree in four years. While it is unclear how much a college education actually serves to improve work productivity, it is clear that a college degree is a necessary requirement for entering most high-paying occupations. Assuming that employers can eventually distinguish between low- and high-ability employees, the most able individuals then have the greatest incentive to complete their degree quickly so that they can reap the rewards to high wage growth in these occupations.[18] Second, the most able students may have access to greater financial aid, via merit scholarships or higher family income that permits them to focus on their studies. Finally, less able students may find college work relatively more onerous than do more able students and so prefer to spend relatively more time on other activities, like work.

With this in mind, we now turn back to the NLSY data to investigate how AFQT scores correlate with work intensity while in school and what that means for college completion rates. Table 3.2 lists mean annual hours of work per year for those currently attending school by AFQT category. The table shows a drop from 991 to 883 to 732 annual hours of work across AFQT Categories IIIA, II, and I individuals in the 1997 cohort; a similar decline in mean annual hours worked across AFQT categories is observed in the 1979 cohort. Curiously, there is an increase in annual hours of work for Category IIIA relative to IIIB.

---

[18] The idea here is that employers use a college degree as a screening device when making initial hires. There is considerable heterogeneity in ability within the population of college graduates, however, and, eventually, an employee's type is revealed through his or her on-the-job experience. High-ability individuals have an incentive to reveal their type as soon as possible, whereas low-ability individuals do not. Moreover, we might expect the incentive for a high-ability individual to reveal his or her type to increase as the overall quality of the college signal deteriorates as more and more individuals seek a college degree. Starting pay for a college graduates may fall, while long-run returns to ability increase.

Table 3.2

Annual Hours Worked in 1983 and 2001 for Currently Enrolled Individuals by AFQT Category

AFQT Category	1979	1997
I	810	732
II	930	883
IIIA	955	991
IIIB	848	884
IVA	973	929

Notes: Sample restricted to individuals currently enrolled in college ages 19 to 21 in 1983 and 2001. See text for explanation of AFQT category.
SOURCES: 1979 and 1997 NLSY.

As noted above, the negative correlation between AFQT score and annual hours of work among enrolled individuals could reflect the effects of both ability and family background. That is, individuals with relatively low AFQT scores might work while in college because their comparative advantage is in work and because family resources are insufficient to cover their expenses while in school. In an effort to disentangle these two mechanisms, we implemented a linear regression of annual hours of work in 2001 based on AFQT score, age, gender, race, school type, and mother's education. Mother's education serves as a proxy for family resources. The regression (see Table 3.3) reveals an independent, but statistically insignificant, negative effect of AFQT on annual hours of work while in school. In column (2) of Table 3.3, we restrict the sample to individuals enrolled in a four-year college. Here we see a robust negative effect of AFQT on annual hours of work, suggesting that relatively less able students work more while in school, regardless of family resources.

Table 3.3

AFQT, Hours of Work, and College Completion Rates: OLS Results

	Dependent Variable			
	Annual Hours Worked: 1997 Cohort			2 or 4 Year Degree Completion: 1979 Cohort
	(1)	(2)		(3)
AFQT	-0.730	-2.147		0.004
	(0.841)	(0.996)		(0.0004)
Male	-38.851	-78.839		-0.029
	(36.195)	(41.816)		(0.018)
Black	-120.732	-148.975		-0.066
	(55.878)	(73.440)		(0.025)
Hispanic	-177.300	-237.295		-0.092
	(49.099)	(56.438)		(0.028)
Four-year college	-311.019	—		0.143
	(42.207)			(0.018)
Mother's education				
High school	59.334	106.206		0.003
	(57.905)	(73.574)		(0.023)
Some college	1.893	72.038		-0.007
	(58.809)	(73.526)		(0.030)
College	-143.122	-70.412		0.079
	(59.626)	(71.791)		(0.032)
Constant	1171.914	923.230		0.171
	(75.877)	(98.317)		(0.420)
N	1343	995		2,601
R^2	0.073	0.048		0.181

Notes: Dependent variable in (1) and (2) is annual hours of work in 2001; dependent variable in (3) is dichotomous variable equal to one if respondent completed degree within six years of initial enrollment. AFQT in (1) and (2) is derived using principal components as explained in the text. Mother's education is measured in 1997 and 1979, respectively. Specifications (1) and (2) control for age in 2001. Specification (3) controls for age at enrollment. Sample is restricted to individuals enrolled in college. Specification (2) is restricted to those enrolled in four-year college institutions. See text for further sample restrictions. Standard errors are in parentheses.
SOURCES: 1979 and 1997 NLSY.

It is also apparent that higher AFQT individuals complete their college degrees more rapidly than lower AFQT individuals. We see this in Table 3.4, which shows college completion rates by AFQT category for the 1979 cohort. We have not observed the 1997 cohort for long enough to perform this tabulation. The sample is restricted to individuals ages 15 to 19 in 1979 who enrolled in either a two- or four-year college program between ages 17 and 21 and whom we observe in the data at least six years later. The table shows a steady decline in college completion rates across AFQT categories. For example, the percentage of individuals who enrolled in a four-year degree program and completed a bachelors degree within six years declines from 84 percent among Category I individuals to 39 percent among Category IIIB individuals. We see similar gradients over four- and five-year time intervals. Completion rates are uniformly low among individuals enrolling in a two-year program, which are favored by lower AFQT individuals (see the first column of Table 3.4). Thus, overall college completion rates for Category IIIA and IIIB individuals are quite low. Within six years, only 33 percent of Category IIIA individuals and 31 percent of Category IIIA and IIIB individuals who enrolled in either a two- or four-year college program had completed an associates degree or more.

Table 3.4

College Completion Rates by AFQT Category: 1979 Cohort

AFQT Category	Fraction in 4-year college	Fraction finished 2-Year Degree in				Fraction finished 4-Year Degree in		
		4 years	5 years	6 years		4 years	5 years	6 years
I	0.83	0.28	0.38	0.45		0.54	0.76	0.84
II	0.65	0.22	0.34	0.39		0.33	0.53	0.60
IIIA	0.53	0.16	0.24	0.29		0.29	0.41	0.47
IIIB	0.51	0.17	0.20	0.25		0.18	0.33	0.39
IVA	0.44	0.17	0.19	0.21		0.12	0.14	0.19

Notes: Sample restricted to individuals between the ages of 15 and 19 in 1979, enrolled in college between ages 17 and 21, and observed in data at least six years after enrollment.
SOURCE: 1979 NLSY.

We continue to find a positive relationship between AFQT and college completion when we control for family resources using mother's education as a proxy variable. We implement a linear regression where the dependent variable is a dichotomous variable equal to one if the individual completed a two- or four-year degree within six years of enrollment and the independent variables are AFQT score, age at enrollment, gender, race, school type, and mother's education. The results, shown in column (3) of Table 3.3, reveal a strong statistically significant positive effect of AFQT on college completion rates, suggesting that ability matters independent of family resources. Regardless of the mechanisms at work, it is clear from Tables 3.2-3.4 that high AFQT individuals pursue college more intensively than low AFQT individuals. Time to college completion is rising in the general population (National Library of Education 1999), and while many factors have no doubt contributed to this secular increase, it seems likely that the increasing fraction of college attendees with relatively low AFQT scores is part of the explanation.

3.3 SUMMARY

In Chapter 2 we showed that the demand for college has increased throughout the AFQT distribution including Category IIIA and IIIB individuals, the population heavily recruited by the Reserves. As we will show in the next section, educational benefits appeal to this population—but what kind of educational benefits? We argued in this section that Category III individuals do not pursue college as intensively as Category I and II individuals. Indeed, fewer than one-third of Category III individuals finish a two- or four-year degree program within six years of their initial enrollment and, no doubt, many of these individuals will never finish. This fact suggests that either Category III individuals have trouble completing their college studies because they must work intensively in order to finance their college education or, conversely, they work intensively because the returns to receiving a college degree for them are comparatively low and their prospects of completing college are low. The fact that AFQT score has an effect on work effort and college-completion rates independent of family resources hints that the latter explanation may drive college behavior in this population. We will argue in Chapter 5 that this observation suggests that educational benefits in the Reserves are already tailored to individuals who pursue college less intensively and that any restructuring of benefits should be targeted to those who wish to pursue college more intensively, namely those in AFQT Categories I and II.

CHAPTER FOUR EDUCATIONAL BENEFIT OPPORTUNITIES IN THE RESERVES

The real cost of attending a two- or four-year postsecondary educational institution rose considerably over the late 1980s and 1990s. Tuition and fees at four-year colleges nearly doubled from $2,200 in 1985 to about $4,000 in 2000; the real cost of tuition and fees at two-year institutions increased from about $900 to $1,300 over the same period (U.S. Bureau of the Census, 2002). As these costs have risen, reservists and civilians alike have come to rely more heavily on grants and subsidized loans to finance their college education. This section reviews the principal kinds of educational benefits available to reservists and provides information on their usage and on reservists' level of satisfaction with those benefits. The section also compares financial aid received by reservists and non-reservists. These comparisons provide one measure of the adequacy of current educational benefits available to reservists and how restructured educational benefits might fit into the menu of available benefits.

4.1 EDUCATIONAL BENEFITS AVAILABLE TO RESERVISTS

Reservists are entitled to educational benefits by virtue of either their active duty service or their reserve duty service. Currently, all prior service reservists are eligible to receive MGIB benefits providing they contribute $1,200 toward their benefits during their first year of service and satisfactorily complete their service obligation. While active members can use MGIB benefits to attend college while they serve on active duty, all but a small fraction of recipients use their benefits after they have left active duty.[19] Many prior service members are also entitled to College Fund benefits available to high-quality recruits who enlist in a critical skill area in the active components of the Army, Navy, or Marine Corps (the Air Force does not have a college fund program). College Fund benefits supplement MGIB benefits. While the

---

[19] Of the 1.7 million individuals receiving MGIB-Active Duty benefits in July 2002, only 6,500 were currently on active duty. These figures were taken from the DMDC Information Delivery System.

dollar amount of these benefits varies across services and occupations, the current maximum lifetime benefit, representing the sum of MGIB and College Fund benefits, is $50,000.

By virtue of their reserve service, reservists are also entitled to receive MGIB-SR benefits. Reservists who are eligible for both the MGIB and MGIB-SR cannot use them simultaneously, only sequentially. In FY 2003, MGIB-SR benefits paid up to $276 per month toward college tuition and room and board for up to 36 months. To be eligible for MGIB-SR benefits, reservists must assume a six-year selected reserve obligation and have completed initial training. The MGIB-SR program also requires reservists to possess a high school diploma or equivalent certificate before completing initial training. The lifetime maximum MGIB-SR benefit was $9,936 in FY 2003. Reservists assigned to critical skill areas or units are eligible to receive supplemental MGIB-SR benefits (a "kicker") that raise the monthly benefit to a maximum of $626 and the maximum lifetime benefit to $22,536. Table 4.1 summarizes the main features of the MGIB and MGIB-SR programs.

The Reserves will also repay some federal student loans for qualified reservists. Federal loans that qualify for repayment include the Stafford Loan Program, the Federal Insured Student Loans, and the Perkins Loan. The reserve components differ in the maximum amount of loan repayment they offer. The Army will repay loans up to $20,000 for a non-prior service reserve enlistment in critical skill areas, while the Air Force Reserve will repay loans up to $15,000 per member or three annual payments of $5,000, depending on whether the reservist is prior or non-prior service. The Naval Reserve Coast Guard and the Marine Corps did not offer loan repayment in 2003. To qualify for the loan repayment program an Army reservist must be high quality, have a six-year reserve obligation, and enlist in particular skill areas or units experiencing supply shortages. The annual loan repayment amount for the Army Reserve is $1,500 for each year of service or 15 percent of the outstanding principal balance of the loan, whichever is greater (see Table 4.2).

Table 4.1

Features of Educational Benefits for Reservists, MGIB, and MGIB-SR: FY 2003

	MGIB[a]	MGIB-Selected Reserve[c]

Amount	Contribute $1,200 in first year
	
	Maximum benefit for:
	  2-year enlistment: $26,352
	  3-6 year enlistment: $32,400
		$9,936 maximum benefit

Duration	Paid over 36 months for full-time students	Paid over 36 months for full-time students
Eligibility Requirements	High school diploma or equivalent Non-prior service recruit or only have Inactive Duty for Training and entered active duty for the first time prior to 1985 Must complete 2 years active duty to receive benefits while in service;[b] For a 3-6 year enlistment, must complete 3 years of active duty and have honorable discharge if use benefits after leaving service	Sign a 6-year enlistment contract Complete Initial Active Duty for Training High School diploma or equivalent Remain in good standing in a Selected Reserve Unit

[a]Qualified personnel can also be eligible for additional benefits through the college fund.

[b]Public Law 106-419 (November 2000) reduced from three to two years the obligated service needed for full benefits under the MGIB for those claiming benefits while still on active duty.

[c]Qualified personnel can also be eligible for additional benefits through the MGIB-SR kicker.

Tuition assistance is also currently offered by most reserve components with the terms of this assistance varying in terms of the maximum monthly and annual benefit (see Table 4.3). The Army National Guard will pay up to 75 percent of tuition and fees, up to a maximum of $200 per semester hour. In addition, some states offer tuition incentives for Guard members that vary in their dollar amount. The Army Reserve offers to pay as much as 100 percent of tuition and fees in postsecondary educational institutions, with a maximum of $187.50 per semester hour and $3,500 annually. The Air National Guard offers 75 percent tuition assistance, up to a maximum of $187.50 per semester hour and $1,000 annually. The Air Force Reserve and the Coast Guard Reserve both pay 100 percent of tuition and fees, up to a maximum of $250 per semester hour and up to $4,500 annually per member. The Marine Corps Reserve and the Naval Reserve do not offer tuition assistance.[20]

Table 4.2

Features of the College Loan Repayment Program for Reservists: FY 2003

Maximum Amount	Army Reserve: $20,000 Army Guard: $10,000 Air Reserve: $15,000 Air Guard: $20,000
Payments	15 percent of outstanding principle balance on the loan annually, or $1,500, whichever is greater, for each year of service
Qualifying Loans	Auxiliary Loan Assistance for Students Stafford Student Loan Parents Loans for Undergraduate Students Consolidated Loan Program Federally Insured Student Loans Perkins Loans
Eligibility Requirements	Must enlist for 6 years Army: Must enlist in specific shortage occupation May have to give up MGIB eligibility

---

[20] Members of the Army Reserve and the Naval Reserves are eligible for active duty tuition assistance if they are currently on active duty. Specifically, they can receive benefits up to 100 percent of their postsecondary education tuition and fees up to a maximum of $250 per semester credit hour and a $4,500 FY maximum. The Navy limits the tuition assistance benefit to 12 semester hours per FY rather than $4,500 per year.

Table 4.3

Features of Undergraduate Tuition Assistance for Reservists: FY 2003

	Amount Covered
Air Force Reserve	100% of tuition and fees up to $250 per semester hour, or $166.67 per quarter hour, up to $4,500 annually
Air National Guard	75% of tuition assistance up to $187.50 per semester hour or $125 per quarter hour up to $1,000 annually
Army Reserve	100% of tuition assistance up to $187.50 per semester hour or $125 per quarter hour up to $3,500 annually
Army Guard	75% of tuition assistance up to $200 per semester hour or $133 per quarter hour up to $4,000 annually
Coast Guard Reserve	100% of tuition assistance up to $250 per semester hour or $166.67 per quarter hour up to $4,500 annually

4.2 THE ADEQUACY OF EDUCATIONAL BENEFITS IN THE RESERVES

Whether the Reserves should consider experimenting with a College-First type program hinges to some extent on the adequacy of current educational benefits offered by the Reserves. There is, of course, no simple measure of adequacy. From a pure efficiency standpoint, an adequate educational benefit would be one that, combined with other pecuniary and non-pecuniary reserve benefits like pay and retirement benefits, maximizes high-quality accessions at minimum cost. We cannot, in the context of this project, assess adequacy by this criterion. We can, however, more crudely examine the extent to which current reserve benefits cover tuition and fees at two- and four-year college and universities[21] and compare the level of educational benefits reservists receive with those received by civilians and active duty members. We can also tabulate survey data that directly queries reservists on how satisfied they are with their educational benefits. While certainly not

---

[21] The DoD biennial report to Congress on the MGIB used this measure to judge the adequacy of the MGIB benefit. For example, see OSD (1996).

definitive, these measures of adequacy provide us with a general sense of whether reservists can expect to receive levels of financial aid comparable to what they might receive as civilians or active duty members and whether they think these benefits are reasonable.

4.2.1 Comparison of Reserve Financial Aid with College Costs

Simple comparisons suggest that reserve educational benefits are sufficient to cover the cost of fees and tuition at most two- and four-year public universities. In the 1999-2000 academic year, mean tuition and fees at two- and four-year public universities and colleges totaled $822 and $3,307 per academic year.[22] The MGIB-SR alone provided reservists with a maximum benefit of $2,405 in 2000. MGIB-SR kicker benefits and tuition assistance for qualified reservists would easily cover the remainder. For example, a reservist qualified for MGIB-SR kicker benefits could receive a maximum of $5,556 in 2000. Prior service members, of course, could use their active duty MGIB benefits and receive even higher levels of financial aid. Reserve benefits would most likely not cover the cost of attending the typical private four-year college or university; tuition and fees at these institutions averaged $12,331 in the 1999-2000 academic year. Room and board at four-year institutions averaged about $8,400 in 1999-2000. Earlier in the introduction to this section we noted that the mean real cost of attending any two- or four-year institution was $1,300 and $4000, respectively.

4.2.2 Comparison of Reserve Financial Aid with Civilian and Active Duty Financial Aid

It is a relatively simple matter to compare the financial aid received by reservists with that received by civilians and active duty personnel, but inferring what those comparisons imply about adequacy is complicated by a number of factors. First and foremost, we must recognize that individuals who choose to affiliate with the Reserves and active duty are different from those who do not in a number of unobservable ways. Thus, simple comparisons across groups will not

---

[22] Authors' calculation from the 2000 NPSAS.

necessarily tell us what kind of financial aid a given reservist would have received had he or she remained a civilian or joined the active force. A second complication is that the terms of financial aid vary greatly by source. In the Reserves and for active duty, of course, financial aid is contingent on assuming the responsibilities and risks of being a member of the armed services. Civilians, for the most part, do not assume those risks. Of particular concern to reservists is the possibility that their college studies could be interrupted by activation.

Additionally, there are many different sources of financial aid available to reservists, active duty members, and veterans. These sources include federal aid programs, such as the Pell Grant program, the Perkins loan program, and work-study programs, as well as state-provided aid and institutional-based aid. Aid provided by states and by educational institutions were among the fastest growing sources of college financial aid in the 1990s (Fair, 2003). Reservists and active duty members do not necessarily forgo these sources of civilian financial aid. Financial aid programs usually differ in specific details as well. For example, the maximum dollar value of the benefits will differ across source, as will eligibility criteria. Some civilian programs determine eligibility based on financial need while others determine eligibility based on merit and scholastic achievement. Also, some benefits are in the form of grants, while others are in the form of loans that must be repaid at a later date.

In the case of military benefits, the two major programs, the MGIB for active duty members and the MGIB-SR for Selected Reserve members, have significantly different benefit structures. As noted earlier in this section, active duty members must contribute $1,200 toward their MGIB benefits during their first year of service; the MGIB-SR requires no such contribution. The timing of when members can receive benefits also differs. Reservists are entitled to receive benefits after they complete initial training, which typically takes no more than a few months. Active duty members, on the other hand, must complete at least two years of their service obligation prior to receiving benefits and, even then, most active duty members will find it difficult to use their

MGIB benefits until after they separate (i.e., become veterans). As Tables 4.2 and 4.3 demonstrate, tuition assistance and loan repayment programs vary significantly across reserve components. Active duty tuition assistance programs are required by Congress to be identical across the active components.

Rather than attempting to calculate what a typical reservist, active duty member, or civilian might receive in financial aid by using program benefit formulas and eligibility requirements, we rely on the 2000 NPSAS that collected data on total grants and loans received from all sources by a nationally representative sample of students attending undergraduate institutions in the academic year 1999-2000.[23] The financial aid data were collected from both administrative sources and students themselves. Importantly, the survey permits us to identify separately non-veteran civilians, veteran civilians, active duty personnel, and reservists. The reader is cautioned that while the comparisons we present below provide a sense of how reservists, active duty members, and civilians fare in terms of financial aid, they do not tell us what a typical reservist would receive in financial aid were he or she to seek that aid from civilian sources alone. We return to this point below.

Figure 4.1 shows the mean level of financial aid received in academic year 1999-2000 by undergraduates ages 19 to 30 who are civilians, current active duty members, reservists, or veterans according to source of aid: grant, loan, or VA/DoD-provided funding. The figure shows that reservists and veterans receive roughly comparable levels of total aid, about $4,770 per year.[24] Active duty members appear to earn less financial aid, although once they separate, they appear to

---

[23] Grants include federal, state, and institutional grants, employer reimbursements, and grants from other private sources. State grants include grants attributable to National Guard service. Loans include federal, state, institutional, and private commercial loans. Loans exclude PLUS loans received by parents for educational purposes.

[24] The differences across civilians, reservists, and veterans observed in the figure are not statistically significant at conventional levels. Total aid is just the simple sum of grants, loans, and VA/DOD-provided aid. We make no adjustments to the value of loan aid to account for the fact that it must eventually be repaid.

earn comparable levels of financial aid. For reservists, total financial aid is approximately equally distributed among grants, loans, and VA/DoD sources.[25] State sources (including state grants to National Guardsmen) are small in comparison to federal aid. The typical reservist receives $192 from state sources and $1,740 from Federal (non-VA/DOD) sources while the typical civilian receives $325 from state sources and $2,191 from Federal (non-VA/DOD) sources. Reservists, though, receive an additional $1,425 from VA/DOD sources while civilians receive virtually nothing from those sources. Civilians, on the other hand, receive higher levels of financial aid from institutional sources than do reservists.

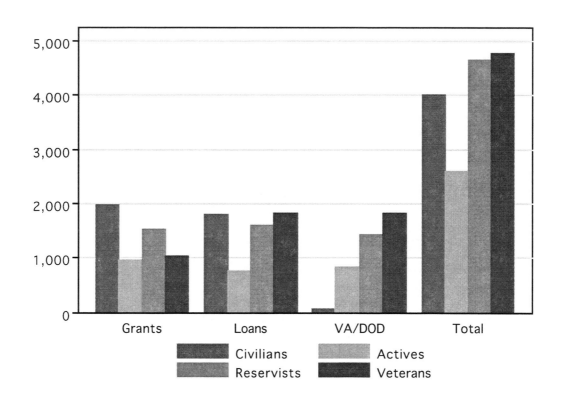

Figure 4.1 Financial Aid Received Academic Year 1999-2000 by Source, Undergraduates, Ages 18 to 30

SOURCE: 2000 NPSAS.

---

[25] Reservists may be eligible for VA educational benefits, and specifically the MGIB, as a result of service performed on active duty.

Uptake of educational benefits has increased somewhat over time in the Reserves. Using the 1986, 1992, and 2000 RCS, we compute the fraction of reservists between the ages of 19 and 30 who are currently using varying forms of VA/DOD-provided financial aid. Figure 4.1 shows the percentage of reservists using active duty-related educational benefits such as the MGIB, the percent using the MGIB-SR program, and the percent using state-provided educational benefits provided to Guard members. The right-most columns in the figure show the percentage receiving any military-related educational benefit. The figure shows that 70 percent of reservists ages 19 to 30 reported that they were currently receiving at least one form of financial aid from military sources in 2000. Owing to a substantial jump in MGIB-SR usage between 1986 and 1992 from 24 percent to 56 percent,[26] the percent of reservists receiving any benefit rose from 55 percent in 1986 to 73 percent in 1992 and then declined slightly to 70 percent in 2000.

Figure 4.2 indicates that state benefits from the National Guard are a relatively minor source of financial aid for reservists. The RCS data indicate that most prior service reservists rely on their active duty benefits rather than the MGIB-SR (77 percent of prior service respondents reported using active duty benefits and 23 percent of prior service respondents reported using MGIB-SR benefits). The low usage of the MGIB-SR among prior service members no doubt is due to the fact that the MGIB and College Fund provide higher monthly benefits than does the MGIB-SR. Furthermore, reservists who are eligible for both the MGIB and MGIB-SR cannot use them simultaneously, only sequentially.

---

[26] Both the MGIB and MGIB-SR were established in October 1984 and cover members who first entered active duty or who enlisted, reenlisted, or extended an enlistment with a Selected Reserve Component after June 30, 1985 (DoD Office of the Actuary, 2001).

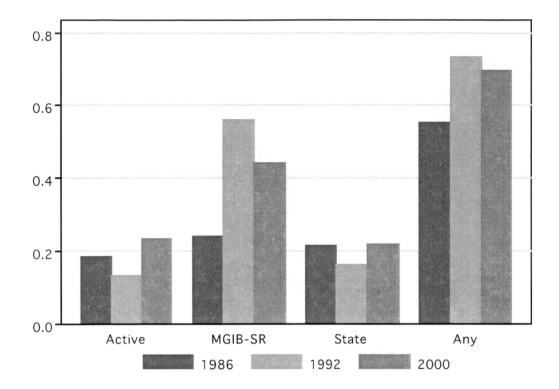

Figure 4.2 Fraction of Currently Enrolled Reservists Ages 19 to 30 Using Educational Benefits

SOURCE: 1986, 1992, and 2000 RCS.

4.2.3 Comparing MGIB and MGIB-SR Benefits

Recently, Congress has expressed concern that the MGIB-SR program treats reservists unfairly relative to the MGIB benefits available to active duty members. As part of this project, RAND was asked to evaluate whether these programs treat reservists inequitably.[27]

Figure 4.3 shows that the maximum monthly benefit under the MGIB clearly exceeds that available under the MGIB-SR program. In 2004, the monthly MGIB benefit was $985 and the monthly MGIB-SR benefit was $282.

---

[27] This analysis focuses on the equity rather than the relative cost-effectiveness of these programs. An analysis of cost-effectiveness would consider the effects of these programs on active and reserve accessions, attrition, and retention (and therefore expected man-years or duty days) as well as cost. Since producing estimates of the marginal effects of MGIB-SR on reserve accessions was beyond the scope of our study, we were unable to estimate relative cost-effectiveness.

Benefits have grown over time under both programs, with the MGIB-SR benefit rising steadily and growth in the MGIB benefit accelerating after 1999. The MGIB has consistently provided greater monthly benefits than the MGIB-SR and the gap in benefits has risen since 1999.

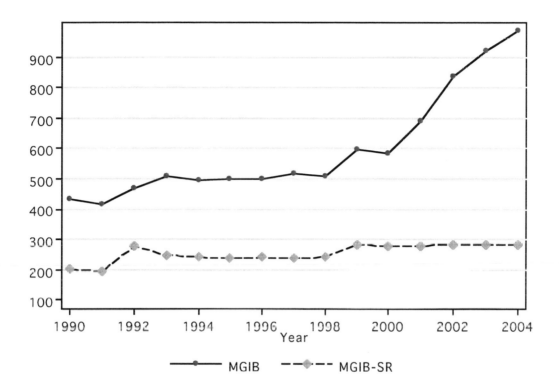

Figure 4.3 Maximum Monthly MGIB and MGIB-SR Benefit, Constant 2004 Dollars

SOURCE: DoD Actuary, OSD-Compensation.

This comparison of maximum monthly benefits, however, ignores the fact that reservists are eligible to receive their MGIB-SR benefits immediately while active duty members typically must wait until they have separated from active duty or, at least, have completed one term of enlistment. The appropriate comparison, then, should account for the different timing of benefit receipt under the MGIB and MGIB-SR programs, the fact that some active duty members will fail to complete their service obligation and therefore will be ineligible to receive MGIB benefits, and the fact that active duty members must make a contribution toward their MGIB benefits. We therefore compute and compare the expected present discounted value (PDV) of the MGIB and MGIB-SR programs, taking into account these program differences. The PDV concept allows us to compare what a given stream of potential future MGIB benefits is worth today. The PDV computations are from the perspective of a twenty-year-old, non-prior service enlistee. Additional assumptions we use to make these PDV computations are described in Appendix A.

We find that the PDV of educational benefits provided by the MGIB-SR program exceeds the PDV of educational benefits provided by the MGIB until 2002 (Figure 4.4). Thus, a potential recruit considering the value of MGIB benefits associated with reserve versus active duty service would find expected MGIB benefits higher in the Reserves until 2002. The main reason why the PDV of the MGIB-SR is higher for reservists, despite the fact that the monthly benefit is smaller, is that the typical active duty member does not begin to receive the MGIB benefit until four years after initial enlistment. Young adults discount future benefits at a high rate (we assume a discount rate of 15 percent), so the value of future benefits like the MGIB is much less than the value of current benefits like the MGIB-SR. In FY 2002, we find that the MGIB benefits are higher, not lower, than MGIB-SR benefits. The reason for the switch is the large increase in monthly MGIB benefits from $650 per month in 2001 to $800 in 2002.[28]

Although the present value of reserve benefits is smaller than under the active program, is this result necessarily unfair? On the criteria of comparability, or equal pay for equal work, the answer depends on whether one believes reservists and active duty members actually perform equal work. Although today reservists are called upon more than ever to perform the same duties and take the same risks as active duty members, there are still a number of ways in which reserve and active duty service differ. The most important may be that non-activated reserve duty involves fewer days of service and has a relatively predictable and limited routine—a weekend of drilling each

_____

[28] Assuming a higher personal discount rate of 20 percent leads to a similar result, except the crossover point occurs two years later, in FY 2004 rather than in FY 2002 (see Appendix B, Figure B.1).

month and two weeks of training in the summer. Active duty service requires full-time duty and often involves long, irregular hours. Also, active duty members and their families are relocated every few years under permanent change of station moves, whereas reservists are not subject to such moves. Such moves can have a negative effect on the earnings of military spouses. Clearly both active and reserve duty have increased for the recent operations in Afghanistan and Iraq, and for the war on terrorism. Many of the recent reserve deployments have been long—arguably much longer than reservists might have expected. Because of the differences in the reserve and active professions, it is not entirely unclear how to weigh the educational benefits available to active and reserve personnel. From the standpoint of the dollar value of the benefits, our comparisons of the PDV of future benefits indicate that MGIB-SR benefits are generally adequate, although, beginning in 2002, the value of MGIB benefits for active members have edged higher than the value of MGIB-SR benefits for reservists.[29]

---

[29] With the activations of reservists and guard members for extended periods of time since September 11, 2001, the question arises whether members can be eligible for and/or receive both MGIB and MGIB-SR benefits. Reservists who qualify for MGIB-SR benefits and who are activated under Title 10 of the U.S. Code and serve continuously for two years on active duty can be eligible for the MGIB. However, like active duty members, they must contribute $1,200 and have honorable service. Individuals cannot receive MGIB and MGIB-SR payments simultaneously and cannot use the same service to qualify for both benefits. However, they can receive payments at different times.

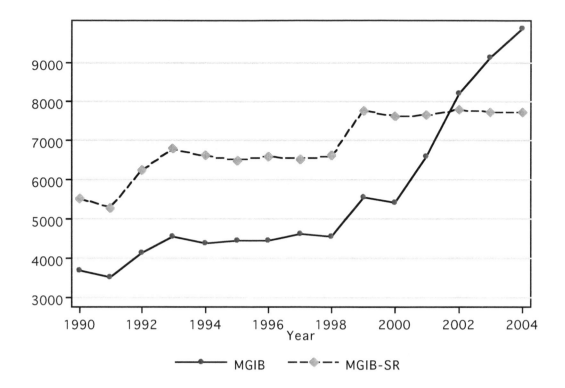

**Figure 4.4 Expected Present Discounted Value of MGIB and MGIB-SR
Benefits in Constant 2002 Dollars**

SOURCE: DoD Actuary, OSD-Compensation, and authors' computations

4.2.4 How Reservists View the Adequacy of Educational Benefits

Another way to assess the adequacy of educational benefits
available to reservists is to consider how satisfied reservists are with
these programs relative to other forms of pecuniary and non-pecuniary
benefits of reserve duty. Figure 4.5 shows the percentage of reservists
ages 19 to 30 surveyed in 2000 who report a given factor was a great or
very great influence on their decision to stay in the Reserves,
categorized by whether the reservist was enrolled in school. For those
enrolled in school, educational benefits were clearly the most important
factor influencing their decision to stay. We find that 67 percent of
those enrolled indicated that educational benefits had a great or very
great influence on their decision to stay. The next most frequently
cited reason for staying (56 percent of respondents) was service to
country. We also find that 43 percent of reservists who are not enrolled
in school report that educational benefits had a great or very great

influence on their decision to stay in the Reserves. Thus, even the
option of receiving educational benefits has an important influence on
retention decisions. In terms of the other factors that are listed, such
as training and pride in service, there are no detectable differences in
the responses of those enrolled relative to those not enrolled in
school. Interestingly, the financial benefits of reserve service such as
income, retirement, and bonuses were cited by relatively few reservists
ages 19 to 30. For example, only about 20 percent of reservists stated
that bonuses had a great or very great influence on their decision to
stay in the Reserves. In short, Figure 4.5 suggests that educational
benefits factor heavily in the retention decisions of young reservists.

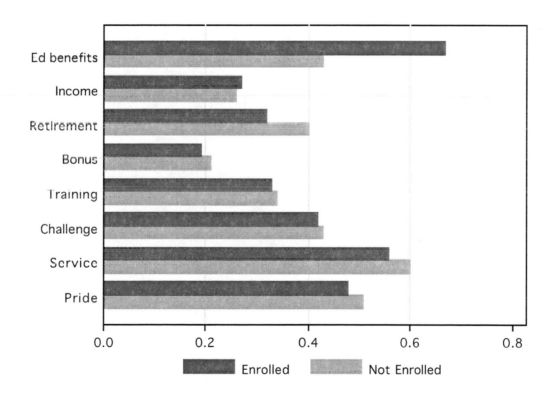

**Figure 4.5 Percent of Reservists, Ages 18 to 30, Reporting that Factor
Was Great or Very Great Influence on Decision to Stay in the Reserves**

SOURCE: 2000 RCS.

More directly, reservists were asked to report on their overall
level of satisfaction with various reserve benefits, including

educational benefits. The data indicate that 57 percent of those
reservists currently enrolled in school and 44 percent of those not
enrolled in school report being satisfied with their educational
benefits, while 24 and 20 percent, respectively, report being
dissatisfied with their educational benefits. Thus, the majority of
reservists are satisfied with their educational benefits. The data
indicate further that those reservists who are dissatisfied with their
educational benefits tend to be dissatisfied with other aspects of their
reserve service as well.

4.3 SUMMARY

In this section, we have considered four ways of assessing whether
the current array of educational benefits available to reservists is
adequate. We find that a large fraction of young reservists use their
educational benefits and that reservists are largely satisfied with
their educational benefits and believe these benefits greatly influence
their decision to remain in the Reserves. We also find that the
educational benefits reservists receive are sufficient to cover all or
most of tuition and fees at two- or four-year public universities and
that the total financial aid they receive compares favorably to aid
received by civilians and veterans of active duty service. We also find
that the present discounted value of MGIB-SR benefits have, in the past,
compared favorably to the present discounted value of benefits provided
to active members through the MGIB program.

The adequacy of current educational benefit programs offered by
the reserve components should also be judged on how cost-effective they
are in attracting and retaining qualified personnel, a topic not
addressed in this analysis. In addition, it is important to recognize
that these present discounted value calculations ignore other
considerations that likely affect how service members actually value
MGIB and MGIB-SR benefits. For example, if a service member is uncertain
about whether he or she will complete a service obligation or will
qualify for a federal loan, the expected value of educational benefits
may be less than purely financial computations suggest. Nonetheless, the
results of this section suggest that the current menu of educational

benefits available to reservists is valued, is used extensively, and compares favorably to financial aid available to veterans and civilians.

CHAPTER FIVE POLICY IMPLICATIONS

This research is intended as a first step in considering whether the Reserves should restructure the educational benefits they offer in order to enhance incentives for high-quality, college-bound youth to enlist in the Reserves. In this section, we consider this question directly, building on the analyses presented in earlier sections. We begin by briefly reviewing some of the major active duty initiatives in this area, such as the College-First program, to understand how these new programs are making active service more complementary with college attendance. We then consider what a College-First program might look like in the Reserves and discuss under what conditions such programs are likely to enhance reserve recruiting. Ultimately, we believe that the value of these programs in the Reserves depends on two factors: (1) the number and types of individuals the Reserves wish to recruit in the future; and (2) the frequency and duration of activations a reservist can expect in the future. We elaborate on these points in a final subsection.

5.1 ACTIVE DUTY INITIATIVES TO RECRUIT COLLEGE-BOUND YOUTH

Recognizing that colleges and universities were becoming an increasingly intense source of competition for high-quality youth, the active components implemented a number of significant changes to their educational benefit programs beginning in the mid-1990s. These changes included increasing the maximum monthly and annual payouts under the MGIB, College Funds, and tuition assistance programs. The active force also experimented with two recruiting initiatives—the Army's College-First program and the Navy's Tech-Prep program—that specifically targeted high-quality youth who desired to attend college immediately following high school.[30]

---

[30] The active and reserve components offer many opportunities for members to increase their education in addition to the ones mentioned here. A summary of these programs can be found in Thirtle (2001).

The pilot test of the Army's College-First program began in February 2000. The test offered two variants of the College-First program in nationally representative samples of Army recruiting districts. One variant of the program offered qualified high school graduates the opportunity to attend up to two years of college before beginning active duty service. These recruits were placed in the Delayed Entry Program (DEP) and attended college before reporting for basic training. After completing up to two years of college, they entered active duty service at an advanced pay grade, E-4, and received a "high-grad" bonus (up to $12,000 for those recruits with some college). The program paid a monthly stipend that was to be in parity with the monthly stipend paid to Reserve Officer Training Corps (ROTC) participants as well as up to $65,000 in federal loan repayment for qualified soldiers.[31] The second variant of the program offered the same benefits as the first variant, but program participants were required to serve in a drilling reserve unit prior to reporting for active duty rather than being placed in the DEP.

Results from the College-First evaluation suggest that the program has potential as a recruiting incentive. The evaluation examined recruiting effects among four groups: high-quality high school seniors, high school graduates with no college, high school graduates with less than one year of college, and high school graduates with one or more years of college. In the first year of the evaluation, the program increased enlistments only among high school graduates with less than one year of college. Recruiting districts that offered the first variant of the College-First program experienced a 43 percent increase in enlistments of high school graduates with less than one year of college, relative to districts that offered neither variant of the program (Orvis, 2001). Initial results from years two through four of the

_____

[31] The value of the stipend as well as the $65,000 Loan Repayment Program (LRP) offer has varied over the course of the pilot test. In FY 2002, parity with the ROTC stipend was restored following an increase from $150 per month to $250 per month for first-year participants and $350 per month for second-year participants. Eligibility for loan repayment was restored in FY 2003 following its omission in the 2002 legislation that restored parity for the stipend.

evaluation, however, indicate that the program has increased enlistments among all four groups (Orvis, personal communication, 2004).

Districts offering the second variant of the program experienced no increase in enlistments relative to districts that offered neither College-First program. This result was not entirely surprising because, as enacted into law during the first year, the program did not allow recruits who chose the College-First program and were assigned to a drilling reserve unit to earn reserve pay and benefits. Thus, potential recruits interested in reserve service were required to choose between joining the Reserves and earning their reserve pay and benefits or taking the College-First benefits and forgoing their reserve pay and benefits. Since the reserve pay and benefits were worth more, very few chose the variant of the College-First program that mandated reserve service.[32]

The other significant recruiting initiative designed to attract high-quality youth is the Navy's Tech-Prep program. Under this program, eligible high school seniors enlist and enter the Navy's DEP. While still high school seniors, they dually enroll in a local community college and complete college credit, taking technical preparation course work. After high school graduation, they can continue their education at the community college for one or two additional semesters, depending on the college. They then enter the active duty Navy, complete recruit training, and attend Navy training in a technical field related to their college education. The Navy training courses are used to help fulfill the requirements for a two-year degree program. By the end of their first enlistment term, they can expect to have completed an Associates Degree in Science. The Navy has formed partnerships with a large number of community colleges to implement this program.

A related Navy initiative, smaller in scope than the Tech-Prep program, is the Navy's College Assistance Student Head Start (CASH) program for college students or high school graduates who qualify for

---

[32] Although this shortcoming was addressed in subsequent legislation, this variant of College-First was eventually discontinued because the Reserves had little incentive to spend up to two years training these non-prior service recruits only to have them join the active components upon completion of their training.

specific occupational areas, such as nuclear engineering. The CASH
program allows individuals to receive full Navy pay (up to an E-3) and
benefits for 12 months while attending college. As a program targeted to
the Navy's most technical fields, the enlistment standards are
considerably higher and the enlistment term of obligation is longer,
usually six years.

Both the Navy Tech-Prep and CASH programs are similar to the Army's
College-First program in that they provide a path for college-bound
youth to attend college prior to entering the military. In the case of
Tech-Prep, the college phase of the program begins in high school and
ends while individuals are serving on active duty. In the case of the
CASH program, the individual can start college following high school
graduation, but he or she completes the two-year college degree during
the first enlistment term. In the case of the College-First program,
members begin and complete the college phase of the program prior to
serving on active duty.

5.2 THE COMPATABILITY OF COLLEGE ATTENDANCE AND RESERVE SERVICE

The active components have aggressively developed new programs and
expanded existing programs in an effort to increase the compatibility of
active duty service and college attendance. While many reserve
educational benefits have also been expanded, there have been no major
initiatives to restructure these programs or develop new programs that
provide additional paths for reservists to combine reserve duty and
college attendance.

Given what we know about how reservists combine reserve duty,
college attendance, and work (Chapter 3) and what we know about how
reservists perceive existing educational programs (Chapter 4), we argue
in this section that, for most potential reserve recruits, reserve
service is highly compatible with college attendance. Activation aside,
reserve service should not interfere with college attendance, at least
no more than other part-time work. Although the typical reservist
clearly has a high demand for a college education, the typical reservist
does not necessarily have a high demand to attend college intensively.
More than 55 percent of reservists ages 19 to 30 are employed full time

while attending college. This percentage is considerably higher than in the general population. We showed further in Chapter 4 that reservists receive financial aid that is comparable to civilians of the same age, which suggests that lack of aid is not driving the decision to work while in school for reservists. Moreover, reservists appear to be generally satisfied with the level of financial aid they receive. Regression-based evidence in Chapter 3 also supports this contention. Work effort while in school (and time to college completion) is higher among lower AFQT individuals than among higher AFQT individuals holding family resources constant (as proxied by mother's education). While the evidence presented in Chapters 2 through 4 is descriptive in nature, the evidence does not suggest that traditional reserve service, activation notwithstanding, is particularly problematic for most recruits who desire a college education.

Reserve service, though, does entail a risk of activation, a risk that increased steadily over the 1990s and has risen sharply since September 11, 2001. For reservists in highly used but low density skill areas, such as military police, the risk of long and frequent activations is currently high and likely to remain high as the United States continues to pursue the war on terrorism at home and abroad. The risk of a long activation could make reserve service unattractive for youth who wish to pursue college intensively. Activations can be highly disruptive to a reservist's studies, can result in the student being dropped from the college enrollment list, and can result in financial loss if activation occurs in the middle of a semester and if tuition, fees, and other expenses cannot be recouped.

DoD and other federal agencies offer several programs aimed at assisting reservists who must suspend their studies due to activation. For example, the Service Members' Opportunity Colleges (SOC) is a consortium of colleges and universities, service components, and military and veteran associations that provide military members an opportunity to attain a degree while in the military, despite their frequent geographic moves. Additionally, the SOC assists reservists in identifying college administrators who should be contacted in the event of activation and negotiating disposition of financial aid and terms of reinstatement.

Reservists are protected from losing any of their MGIB-SR benefits due to activation. Lenders in federal Title IV loan programs, such as the Federal Perkins Loan Program, are required to automatically postpone student loan repayment during the time that reservists are activated, and borrowers with subsidized federal loans are eligible to have the federal government assume the interest payments on their loans while they are on active duty.[33] While not required, the Department of Education strongly urges colleges and universities to provide refunds of tuition and fees and to provide easy reenrollment for those forced to withdraw from school due to a military activation. In cases where activated reservists have trouble arranging for an appropriate disposition of tuition and fees and terms of reinstatement upon deactivation with a particular college, the SOC will act as an intermediary between the college and reservist and negotiate a solution.

Tabulations from the 2000 RCS suggest that reservists, in the past at least, have experienced some difficulty coordinating schooling and activation, despite the availability of assistance from the SOC. Overall, about 9 percent of reservists between the ages of 19 and 30 surveyed in the 2000 RCS reported that they had ever left a college or training program due to activation (91 percent of these individuals left a university or college and 9 percent left a training program). About half of these reservists stated that they were involuntarily activated. Regardless of why they were activated, 75 percent of reservists who left school for activation stated they were unable to obtain a full or partial refund for tuition and fees. A little more than half of these reservists (56 percent) stated they were unable to get credit for

---

[33] Information about loan relief for students and borrowers affected by military mobilizations is available from the Department of Education (http://www.ifap.ed.gov/dpcletters/GEN0306.html). Information on the disposition of military educational benefits for activated reservists is available from the SOC Web site (http://www.soc.aascu.org/socguard/Disposition.html).

coursework they had partially completed and 38 percent stated that they were unable to reenroll following their activation.

The prevalence of tuition and other administrative problems reported in the 2000 RCS could be due to a lack of awareness that the SOC even existed. Until September 2001, SOC did little to inform activated reservists that they were available to help. According to the SOC, though, this has changed in recent years. For example, the Army Guard now includes SOC advice in materials it provides to members who anticipate being activated.[34] Still, the high percentage of activated reservists who were students and who experienced lost aid, tuition, or credits suggests that outreach efforts on behalf of the SOC as well as cooperation from schools themselves is critical to reducing the burden of activation for activated students.

Even if activated student reservists can avoid financial losses, activation could impose other non-pecuniary losses that are less easily compensated. Perhaps most importantly, activation will typically lengthen, by an uncertain amount, the time necessary to complete a degree. Also, activation disrupts the continuity of academic study. Continuity may be important if particular courses of study are hampered by interruption. Academic and social relationships may also be affected by activation.

Even so, it is not clear whether the typical reservist will view potential interruptions to academic study as a serious problem. Intensity of college attendance has fallen over time as the demand for college has increased. In particular, Chapter 3 showed that Category IIIA and IIIB individuals, who represent 63 percent of all non-prior service reserve recruits, pursue college less intensively than Category I and II individuals. Category IIIA and IIIB individuals are less likely to complete their studies over a given number of years and work far more hours than Category I and II individuals. From the RCS, we also know that reservists in general work much more while attending school than does the civilian population of the same age attending school.

---

[34] Based on personal communication with Mr. Max Padilla, project director, SOC-Guard, on December 15, 2003.

From this evidence, it would appear that many reservists are unlikely to view potential activation as a serious problem with regard to fulfilling their college plans since they will most likely pursue college in a less intensive fashion regardless. However, future potential recruits might view activation as more disruptive. First, if the mean length and frequency of activation rises, along with the uncertainty of when and where that activation will occur, the threat of activation might be perceived more negatively in the future, even by reservists who would not pursue college intensively. Second, higher aptitude individuals are likely to view the potential for disruption to their academic studies more negatively. To the extent that the reserve components seek to recruit more enlisted personnel from AFQT Categories I and II in the future, disruptions to schooling associated with potential reserve activations will be viewed more negatively by the Reserves' target market. In this case, the Reserves might want to consider a restructured program that reduces the extent to which potential activation interferes with college plans.

5.3 HOW MIGHT EDUCATIONAL BENEFTIS IN THE RESERVES BE RESTRUCTURED?

One model for restructuring educational benefits in the Reserves is the current ROTC program. Specifically, enlisted reservists could attend college without the risk of activation for some period of time, say, two years or even as much as four years while they complete training, but would assume an obligation to serve in the Reserves subsequently for, say, an eight year term of enlistment. Because reservists who claim college benefits during the first two years while they are enrolled without the risk of activation might fail to serve the full eight years, it would be important to enforce penalties for premature separation or enforce a prorated repayment of educational benefits for those who separate early. An alternative to a longer enlistment term of eight years could be to lower reserve pay while the reservist is a student during the initial two years. Or, reservists who participate in the program could choose a shorter term of enlistment but agree to a higher risk of activation during that time period. In short, tradeoffs could be made between reserve pay, risk of activation, and term of enlistment.

A drawback of such a program is the inability of the reserve components to activate the participants, a factor that would significantly reduce their value to the Reserves in the short term. The non-deployable status of the participants could adversely affect reserve unit morale if other reserve members view the non-deployable status of program participants as unfair.

Whether such a program makes sense depends on the cost (financial or other) of providing the benefit and the importance of attracting reservists who seek to attend college intensively, such as those in AFQT Categories I and II. Like the Navy's CASH program, this hypothetical restructured program for reservists could be a narrowly defined program that would only be targeted to highly qualified individuals entering critical occupational areas.

5.4 SUMMARY

In summary, our analysis of available data indicates, while ignoring the potential for activation, that unlike active duty service, reserve service is generally compatible with college attendance. We find that young reservists can and do combine their reserve service with schooling and civilian work; they even work more in their civilian jobs while attending school than civilians of a similar age attending school. Activation, however, can disrupt schooling and will be the most disruptive to those who prefer to attend school intensively and continuously. DoD, with the help of the Department of Education and the Department of Veterans' Affairs, has mechanisms that assist reservists whose academic studies are interrupted by activation, helping them to minimize any financial costs and negotiate with college administrators regarding academic credit and reentry following activation. While a large fraction of activated reservists who were students experienced losses in the past, according to the 2000 RCS, the SOC and the service components have enhanced outreach efforts since September 2001 to ensure that members are aware of the aid available to them.

Other costs associated with college disruption are likely to be experienced most significantly by those higher aptitude individuals (Category I and II) who have a strong preference for attending college intensively and continuously. To the extent that specific occupation or technical areas require higher aptitude personnel or to the extent that the reserve components want to improve the overall aptitude of their enlisted force, allowing some reservists to pursue college first and serve in the Reserves subsequently might make sense. One possibility is to create an ROTC-like program for enlisted personnel that would allow individuals to attend college at a two- or four-year institution while serving in a reserve unit, but protects them from the risk of activation. Following their completion of college, these reservists might be required to enlist for a longer term of service or perhaps serve with a higher risk of activation. Whether such a restructured program would be cost-effective relative to other approaches to increasing recruit quality in the Reserves is a topic requiring further research.

APPENDIX A. DATA APPENDIX

In this appendix, we briefly describe the data sets employed in this research and any global sample restrictions we apply in our analyses.

A.1 RCS

The 1986, 1992, and 2000 RCS surveys gathered information about personal and military background, family composition, economic status, preparedness, mobilizations and deployments, retention plans, spouse and member labor force experience, satisfaction with aspects of Guard and Reserve life, and other quality of life issues. Together with the Active Duty Surveys of Members and Spouses, the RCS is intended to provide a comprehensive picture of the total force. For more information on survey methods, sampling frame, and stratification of the RCS, see, for example, Simmons (2001).

We use all three waves of the RCS administered to enlisted personnel. In 1986, 1992, and 2000, the RCS surveyed 44,720, 21,232, and 16,352 enlisted members, respectively. We focus on enlisted members ages 19 to 30 at the time of the survey, which reduces our sample sizes to 21,235, 8,657, and 6,334, respectively. About 82 percent of this sample is male. In some analyses, we focus on reservists currently attending college, reducing our sample sizes to 6,749, 4,071, and 2,798, respectively. We also excluded full-time reserve technicians and the Active Guard Reserve (AGR) from our sample.

A.2 THE RCCPDS

The RCCPDS assembles administrative data on the reserve population reported by each reserve component on a monthly basis. We use the September 1999 master RCCPDS data files in this report, which contain records on 894,320 selected reservists. We restrict our sample to selected enlisted reservists ages 16 or older with no prior service status who began their reserve service in the year prior to September 1999. This leaves us with a sample size of 42,214.

A.3 THE MARCH CPS

The Annual Demographic Survey or March CPS supplement is the primary source of detailed information on income and work experience in the United States. The Annual Demographic Survey is used to generate the annual Population Profile of the United States, reports on geographical mobility and educational attainment, and detailed analysis of monetary income and poverty status. The labor force and work experience data from this survey are used to profile the U.S. labor market and to make employment projections.[35]

The 2000 March CPS contains records for 22,883 individuals ages 19 to 30. In some instances, we further restricted our sample to males (8,380 observations). Additionally, some analyses focus on individuals currently attending college. The CPS records this information only for individuals ages 19 to 24. With this restriction, the 2000 sample size falls to 3,245 males and females enrolled in college.

A.4 THE NLSY

The NLSY79 is a nationally representative sample of 12,686 young men and women who were 14 to 22 years old when they were first surveyed in 1979. These individuals were interviewed annually through 1994 and are currently interviewed on a biennial basis. The survey covers schooling and labor market activity in considerable detail as well as a myriad of other topics ranging from childcare costs to welfare participation. In 1997, the NLSY began interviewing a second cohort of approximately 9,000 American youth who were 12 to 16 years of age as of December 1, 1996. The 1997 cohort is currently interviewed on an annual basis. Important for our purposes, the NLSY administered the ASVAB to both the 1979 and 1997 cohorts.[36]

We restrict our sample to respondents ages 19 to 21 with a high school degree in 1983 or 2001 (the last year of data available in the NLSY97), with valid ASVAB scores. These sample restrictions yield 4,257 respondents in the NLSY79 and 3,379 respondents in the NLSY97.

---

[35] For more information about the March CPS and its history, please refer to http://www.bls.census.gov/cps/ads/adsmain.htm.

[36] For more information about the NLSY, please refer to http://www.bls.gov/nls/home.htm.

A.5 THE NPSAS

The NPSAS is a comprehensive, nationwide study designed to determine how students and their families pay for postsecondary education and to describe demographic and other characteristics of those enrolled. The study is based on a nationally representative sample of students in postsecondary educational institutions, including undergraduate and graduate students and students attending professional programs. Students attending all types and levels of institutions are represented, including public and private not-for-profit and for-profit institutions, less-than-two-year institutions, community colleges, and four-year colleges and universities. We employ data from the 1999-2000 academic year. Each of the NPSAS surveys provides information on the cost of postsecondary education, the distribution of financial aid, and the characteristics of both aided and non-aided students and their families.[37]

In the NPSAS, it is possible to separately identify current reservists, active duty members, and veterans and determine whether the financial aid they received was from VA or DoD sources. The NPSAS 2000 surveyed 12,422 individuals ages 19 to 30. Our sample of current and former military personnel is small. In 2000, the NPSAS contains records for 106 reservists, 285 veterans, and 99 active duty members.

---

[37] For more information on the NPSAS, please refer to http://nces.ed.gov/surveys/npsas/.

APPENDIX B. A COMPARISON OF MGIB AND MGIB-SR PROGRAM BENEFITS

The MGIB and MGIB-SR programs differ in many respects. The MGIB program requires individuals to contribute $1,200 during the first year of service and those who separate from service are not qualified to receive benefits unless they complete a service obligation of three years (or two years for active duty recipients beginning in FY 2001). Furthermore, although qualified service members are allowed to use MGIB benefits while they are serving on active duty, virtually all personnel begin collecting their benefits after they have separated from active duty. For members with a four-year service obligation, this means waiting four years until they can begin receiving MGIB benefits.

In contrast, reservists can qualify for MGIB-SR benefits as soon as they complete initial training. Basic training is about eight weeks and basic skill training can run from eight weeks to over a year, so that initial training varies from four months to over a year.[38] For a potential recruit weighing the benefits of the MGIB and the MGIB-SR, he or she must compare a program that entails personal contributions and deferred benefits versus a program that entails no personal contribution and almost immediate benefits. Comparing MGIB and MGIB-SR benefits, therefore, requires that we account for these programmatic differences.

We account for the differences in payout timing and contribution requirements by computing the expected present discounted value (PDV) of MGIB and MGIB-SR benefits under a set of assumptions. The PDV concept allows us to compare costs and benefits that occur at different points in time. The PDV computation requires that we make an assumption about the rate at which potential recruits discount future benefits. Recent research shows that younger service members have quite high discount rates. That is, they place relatively little value on benefits that occur far into the future. Warner and Pleeter (2001) estimate discount

_____

[38] Most individuals complete their initial training at one time. The exception is individuals who are juniors in high school who affiliate with the Reserves and who split their initial training over two summers and therefore do not begin claiming MGIB-SR benefits until the end of the summer after their senior year in high school.

rates of over 20 percent for junior enlisted personnel. We use a somewhat lower figure of 15 percent and recognize that lower or higher discount rates will change our comparisons. Our computations discount all dollar figures to the month of entry into military service (i.e., the date of enlistment or affiliation).

We assume that potential active duty recruits at the very beginning of military service would enlist for a four-year enlistment term. Although enlistees could begin using the MGIB benefit while on active duty (after completing two years of service), we assume that they do not use benefits until separating from service, and, that upon separation they attend college for four academic years (36 months) using the maximum MGIB benefit. Thus, the PDV of the maximum MGIB benefit is discounted over an eight-year period: four years of enlistment and four academic years of college. Because enlistees can only receive MGIB upon separation from service if they complete three years (see Chapter 4), we computed the expected PDV of MGIB benefits by multiplying the PDV of the MGIB benefit by the probability the enlistee stays in service for three years. We estimate this probability using annual DoD enlisted continuation rates for years of service one to three, obtained from DMDC. Finally, because the MGIB program requires a $100 per month contribution during the first year of service, we compute the PDV of these contributions and subtract them from the PDV of the MGIB benefit.

To compute the PDV of the MGIB-SR benefits, we assume that a potential reserve recruit would attend college for four academic years (or 36 months) using the maximum MGIB-SR benefit while simultaneously completing his or her six-year reserve obligation. Because reservists can generally begin collecting MGIB-SR benefits a few months after affiliation, the PDV of the MGIB-SR benefit is discounted only over the four years the individual attends college. The MGIB-SR does not require service member contributions.

Figure 4.4 in the main text shows the results of our computations. Given our assumptions, we find that the MGIB-SR for reservists provides a larger PDV benefit than does the MGIB for active duty members until FY 2002 and then the PDV of the MGIB exceeds the PDV of the MGIB-SR thereafter. Thus, a potential recruit considering the value of MGIB benefits associated with reserve versus active duty would find that the expected benefits are larger for the Reserves for years before 2002. The main reason why the PDV of the MGIB-SR is higher prior to 2002, despite the fact that the monthly benefit is smaller than the MGIB benefit in those years, is that individuals do not begin receipt of the MGIB benefit until four years after initial entry. Given that young adults discount future benefits at a high rate, the value of the MGIB is less than the value of the MGIB-SR. In FY 2002, we find that the MGIB benefits are higher, not lower than MGIB-SR benefits. The reason for the switch is that MGIB benefits rose from $650 per month to $800 per month.

It is important to note that the magnitudes of the PDV of the MGIB and MGIB-SR we show change with our assumptions concerning the discount rate. If we assume youth have a higher discount rate, the value of the MGIB-SR will increase relative to the PDV of the MGIB. Recent research by Warner and Pleeter (2001) suggests that mean discount rates of enlisted personnel are about 20 percent. Assuming a discount rate of 20 percent, we find that the PDV of the MGIB exceeds the PDV of the MGIB-SR beginning in 2004 rather than 2002, as shown in Figure B.1.

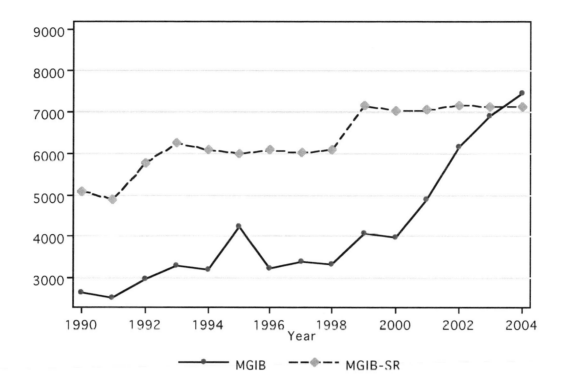

**Figure B.1 Expected Present Discounted Value of MGIB and MGIB-SR
Benefits in Constant 2004 Dollars, Assuming Personal Discount Rate = 20%**

SOURCE: DoD Actuary, OSD-Compensation, and authors' computations

Another factor that could alter our results is the assumption of a
four-year enlistment term. Enlistment terms that are shorter, say three
years, would increase the expected value of the MGIB relative to the
MGIB-SR. On the other hand, decreases in the probability of completing
the first three years of service would reduce the expected value of the
MGIB.

B.1 THE EFFECTS OF INCLUDING COLLEGE FUND AND KICKER BENEFITS

Several of the active components offer an additional college
benefit known as the college fund kicker for high-quality recruits who
enlist in hard-to-fill career fields. The college fund benefit is added
to the MGIB benefit and, importantly, is not adjusted for inflation as
the MGIB and MGIB-SR benefits are. In FY 2004, the maximum college

benefit for the active components is $50,000 over 36 months, of which
$35,460 is MGIB benefits and $14,540 is college fund benefits. Beginning
in 1996, the reserve components could offer a college fund kicker in
addition to the MGIB-SR benefit. Like the active college fund, the
kicker is offered to high-quality personnel entering critical career
fields. The maximum monthly kicker is $350 per month and is currently
offered by the Army Reserve.

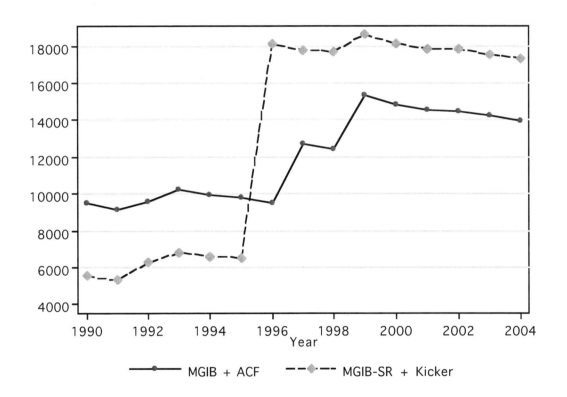

**Figure B.2 Expected PDV of MGIB with College Fund and MGIB-SR with
Kicker, Constant 2004 Dollars**

SOURCES: DoD Actuary, and OSD-Compensation.

To understand how the kickers affect the comparison of the expected
value of the MGIB and MGIB-SR programs, we recomputed our PDV
calculations and included the extra kickers. We assumed individuals
would qualify and use the maximum kicker benefits. Figure B.2 shows the
results. We find that until 1995, adding the college fund kickers
improved the expected PDV of the MGIB program to the extent that the
value of both programs together exceeded the value of the MGIB-SR. The

introduction of the college fund kicker for reserve personnel in 1996 substantially increased the value of the MGIB-SR program to the point that the value of the reserve program far exceeded the value of the MGIB and college fund benefit for active members. However, large increases since 1996 in both the monthly MGIB and college fund benefits resulted in some catch up. Still, the value of the reserve programs (MGIB-SR with kicker) continues to exceed the expected value of the active programs (MGIB with college fund).

B.2 CONCLUSIONS

Our analysis of MGIB and MGIB-SR benefits shows that the MGIB offers higher real monthly benefit levels to recipients of these two programs. Furthermore, the gap in the benefit levels has increased in recent years due to accelerated growth in the MGIB benefit. Thus, from the standpoint of recipients, those receiving MGIB benefits are better off.

However, in addition to being a benefit to active duty members as they transition to veteran status, the MGIB program is also an active duty recruiting tool. Research over many years consistently shows that educational benefits improve the recruitment of high-quality active duty personnel. In addition, the MGIB-SR is a recruitment tool to improve affiliation rates among potential non-prior service reservists. From a recruitment standpoint, comparisons of the MGIB and MGIB-SR programs must account for differences in the programs, particularly in the timing of the payout of benefits and contribution requirements. Accounting for these program differences, we find that the value of the MGIB-SR exceeds the expected value of the MGIB program, until FY 2002 when the value of the MGIB monthly benefit was significantly increased. Once we account for the contributions of the kicker and ACF to the total benefits, we find that the value of the reserve benefit (MGIB-SR with kicker) continues to exceed the value of the active duty benefit (MGIB with ACF).

Importantly, our conclusions could change under alternative assumptions. Worsening continuation rates would reduce the expected value of MGIB benefits, as would a higher assumed discount rate.

The focus of this analysis was on the equity of the value of these benefits. Further analysis is needed of their relative cost-effectiveness. Such an analysis would consider their effects on accessions, attrition, reenlistment, and cost.

REFERENCES

Arkes, Jeremy, and M. Rebecca Kilburn, "Estimates of Reserve Enlistments," Santa Monica, Calif.: RAND Corporation, unpublished draft, 2002.

Asch, Beth J., James R. Hosek, Jeremy Arkes, C. Christine Fair, Jennifer Sharp, and Mark Totten, *Military Recruiting and Retention After the Fiscal Year 2000 Military Pay Legislation,* Santa Monica, Calif.: RAND Corporation, MR-1532-OSD, 2002.

Asch, Beth, Matthias Schonlau, and Can Du, *Policy Options for Recruiting in the College Market: Results from a National Survey,* Santa Monica, Calif.: RAND Corporation, MG-105-OSD, 2003.

Card, David, *Estimating the Return to Schooling: Progress on Some Persistent Econometric Problems,* NBER Working Paper 7769, Cambridge, Mass.: National Bureau of Economic Research, 2000.

Card, David, and John E. DiNardo, "Skill-Biased Technological Change and Rising Wage Inequality: Some Problems and Puzzles," *Journal of Labor Economics,* Vol. 20, No. 4, 2002, pp. 733-783.

Card, David, and Thomas Lemieux, "Can Falling Supply Explain the Rising Return to College for Younger Men? A Cohort-Based Analysis," NBER Working Paper 7655, Cambridge, Mass.: National Bureau of Economic Research, 2000.

DiNardo, J., N. Fortin, and T. Lemieux, "Labor Market Institutions and the Distribution of Wages, 1973-1992: A Semiparametric Approach," *Econometrica,* Vol. 64, No. 5, 1996, pp. 1001-1044.

Fair, C. Christine, "Paying for College: A Survey of Military and Civilian Financial Aid Programs and Postsecondary Education Costs," in M. Rebecca Kilburn and Beth J. Asch, eds., *Recruiting Youth in the College Market: Current Practices and Future Policy Options,* Santa Monica, Calif.: RAND Corporation, MR-1093-OSD, 2003.

Juhn, C., K. Murphy, and B. Pierce, "Wage Inequality and the Rise in Returns to Skill," *Journal of Political Economy,* Vol. 101, No. 3, 1993, pp. 410-442.

Kostiuk, Peter, and James Grogan, *Enlistment Supply into the Naval Reserve,* CRM 87-239, Alexandria, Va.: Center for Naval Analysis, 1987.

MaCurdy, Thomas, and Edward Vytlacil, *Establishing New Norms for the AFQT Using Data from PAY97,* unpublished manuscript, Stanford, Calif.: The Hoover Institution, Stanford University, 2002.

Marquis, Susan, and Sheila Kirby, *Reserve Accessions Among Individuals with Prior Military Service: Supply and Skill Match,* Santa Monica, Calif.: RAND Corporation, R-3892-RA, 1989.

National Library of Education, *College for All? Is There Too Much Emphasis on Getting a 4-year College Degree?* Washington, D.C.: Department of Education, National Library of Education, 1999.

Neal, Derek, and William Johnson, "The Role of Premarket Factors in Black-White Wage Differences," *Journal of Political Economy,* Vol. 104, No. 5, 1996, pp. 869-895.

Orvis, Bruce R., "College First/GED Plus National Recruiting Test: Year One Report," Santa Monica, Calif.: RAND Corporation, unpublished draft, 2001.

Orvis, Bruce R., personal communication with the authors, Santa Monica, Calif.: RAND Corporation, 2004.

Office of the Assistant Secretary of Defense for Reserve Affairs, *Review of Reserve Component Contributions to National Defense,* Washington, D.C., 2002.

Office of the Secretary of Defense, *Biennial Report to Congress on the Montgomery GI Bill Educational Benefit Program,* Washington, D.C.: Office of the Assistant Secretary of Defense, Force Management Policy, 1996.

Segall, Daniel O. *Development and Evaluation of the 1997 ASVAB Score Scale,* unpublished manuscript, Washington, D.C.: Defense Manpower Data Center, 2003.

Shiells, Martha E., *Affiliation of Navy Veterans with the Selected Reserve,* CRM 86-249, Alexandria, Va.: Center for Naval Analyses, 1986.

Simmons, Robert O., *2000 Survey of Reserve Component Personnel: Final Codebook,* Washington, D.C.: Defense Manpower Data Center, 2001.

Tan, Hong, *Non-Prior Service Enlistments: Supply Estimates and Forecasts,* Santa Monica, Calif.: RAND Corporation, R-3786-FMP/RA, 1991.

Thirtle, Michael, *Educational Benefits and Officer-Commissioning Opportunities Available to U.S. Military Service Members,* Santa Monica, Calif.: RAND Corporation, MR-981, 2001.

U.S. Bureau of the Census. *Statistical Abstract of the United States,* Washington, D.C.: U.S. Bureau of the Census, 2002.

Warner, John, and Saul Pleeter, "The Personal Discount Rate: Evidence from Military Downsizing," *American Economic Review,* Vol. 91, No. 1, 2001, pp. 33-53.

Warner, John, Curtis Simon, and Deborah Payne, *Enlistment Supply in the 1990s: A Study of Navy College Fund and Other Enlistment Incentive Programs*, DMDC Report No. 2000-015, Arlington, Va.: Defense Manpower Data Center, 2001.